Engaging the DisEngaged

Beth Critchley Charlton

Pembroke Publishers Limited

For Tom, with love
For Matt and Michèle, with laughter
For Vince, with thanks

© 2010 Pembroke Publishers
538 Hood Road
Markham, Ontario, Canada L3R 3K9
www.pembrokepublishers.com

Distributed in the U.S. by Stenhouse Publishers
480 Congress Street
Portland, ME 04101
www.stenhouse.com

We acknowledge the financial support of the Government of Canada through the Book Publishing Industry Development Program (BPIDP) for our publishing activities.

We acknowledge the assistance of the Government of Ontario through the Ontario Media Development Corporation's Ontario Book Initiative.

Library and Archives Canada Cataloguing in Publication

Charlton, Beth Critchley
    Engaging the disengaged / Beth Critchley Charlton.

Includes index.

ISBN 978-1-55138-258-6

    1. Interaction analysis in education. 2. Effective teaching. 3. Classroom management. I. Title.

LB1034.C44 2010   371.102'2   C2010-903830-4

Editor: Kat Mototsune
Cover Design: John Zehethofer
Typesetting: Jay Tee Graphics Ltd.

Printed and bound in Canada
9 8 7 6 5 4 3 2 1

Mixed Sources
Product group from well-managed forests, and other controlled sources
www.fsc.org Cert no. SW-COC-002358
© 1996 Forest Stewardship Council
FSC

Contents

Introduction: The Disengaged Student

Too many of our students become disengaged from the school experience. We've known this for a long time and we know that it has to change. The question is *what do we do?*

First, it's important that we have a clear sense of who the disengaged student is.

Some students see school as the place that identifies them as not quite "as good as" other students; where they are more aware of what they can't do than what they can do, what is impossible than what is possible, and what is unfair than what is fair. These students often disengage from the schooling process and we often lose them.

Some students, despite all the outward appearances of academic success, disengage from the schooling process as well. For these students, academic success and the ensuing acknowledgments are simply not enough to maintain a sense of engagement. We sometimes lose these students.

Some students complete their school years by flying under the radar: they are present, assignments are completed, and they pass the grade. But being present and completing the work doesn't mean being engaged. These students often spend each school year waiting for it to be over, and some fade away from school altogether.

In short, any student can disengage.

Disengagement from the process of schooling also affects school behavior in a variety of ways. Disengagement can look like passive acceptance or chronic malaise: these students persevere through the years and complete assignments, with results ranging from excellent to mediocre. But it seems they are "doing school," rather than engaging in school.

Disengagement can look like active resistance: these students seem to sabotage the day-to-day procedures in the classroom through disruptive behavior and refusal to complete assignments.

Disengagement can also result in a student's chronic absenteeism or the decision to drop out. As these students see it, school just doesn't seem to offer enough to make engagement in the process worthwhile.

Disengagement isn't usually a constant state. Many students fade in and out of disengagement. In fact, it's the surprising flashes of interest, participation, and exceptionally well-completed assignments that provide us with the confidence that all students are, at times, engaged; it's just the length of that engagement that varies. These moments of re-engagement provide us with enough impetus to work together to figure out how to turn these flashes of short-term engagement into engagement that is sustained.

Some would say there's no excuse for disengaging. Disengagement, they argue, is simply the student's choice to turn off and avoid work. Two solutions to disengagement are often offered. The first is to insist—by means of penalties such as additional homework, detention, and failure—that these students simply get onboard and accept what's offered. After all, the argument goes, school works for everyone else, so why do these kids need something different? Why does this small percentage of students need something different?

The second solution offered is that we should return to the old ways of teaching, in which lessons were delivered, and students behaved and completed their work—or they failed.

Many teachers and I would respond to these proposed solutions in the following ways:

- It's not a small percentage of students who disengage; it's more than we notice and it's a wider population than we think. Just ask your colleagues and friends about their school years. Chances are, many exhibited feelings or signs of disengagement for varying lengths of time. Some persevered, some dropped out, some failed and tried again. That's also true of many of history's great scientific, artistic, mathematical, and dramatic minds.
- In fact, the old ways weren't the panacea many remember. While it's true that there were some models of excellent teaching in "the old days," there were also students who didn't respond to these models—and that's just like today.

We have some excellent models of teaching today, and we continue to have disengaged students. While it's true that there are fewer disengaged students than in the past, we seem to have hit a plateau. Too many students remain disengaged, a clear signal that it's time to acknowledge the evolutionary process of education and to embrace change. It's through that continued evolution that good teachers and good schools foster. They don't go back to the old ways; they acknowledge what we've learned about effective educational practices and build on that foundation of knowledge through research, observation, and conversations.

And it's on that solid foundation that this book rests. We start with an acknowledgment of all that teachers do well and then we embrace the professional conversations that generate questions about the how, the when, and the why of what we do. As we explore these questions, we discuss possibilities, not problems; we acknowledge existing successes, not anticipated failures. The questions lead us to rethinking, and rethinking opens the doors to change; we decide where we want to go and plan together how to get there. Rethinking acknowledges what we've done well and celebrates opportunities to make us better.

It is my hope that this book contributes to these discussions by posing more questions and suggesting some possibilities. If this book provides teachers with an opportunity to acknowledge what they do well and encourages them to have forward-looking conversations about change and exploring ways to rethink some (not all) parts of our professional practice, then this book has accomplished its goal.

It's time to get started. We'll begin with a question that acknowledges our solid foundation. *What do you know?*

1 **What Do You Know?**

Recently, there have been lots of conversation, news items, and research about the disengaged student. With this information comes questions:

- Who are the disengaged students?
- Why are they disengaged?
- What causes their disengagement?
- What can we do about their disengagement?

All questions are worth exploring but, as in any good exploration, we first decide on a place to begin and then we move forward. This book's exploration of disengaged students begins by posing a question that is designed to acknowledge the professional expertise of teachers: *What do you know?*

To answer this question, a teacher reviews what he or she knows about teaching and takes pride in that knowledge. The teacher also welcomes the fact that knowledge it is never static. Knowledge, especially knowledge about teaching and learning, is always open for rethinking.

Each word in this question provides a different perspective on this rethinking: *What do you know?*

What is the word that directs this question. In this book, the "what" refers to the information we accumulate through research and personal experience about how we define and describe disengagement.

Do is a positive word that speaks of ability and possibilities. In this book, "do" refers to the perspective through which we view the student. We look at the student through the lens of "can do" rather than "can't do."

You directs the focus at knowing the individual. In this book, the "you" will sometimes be a student, and sometimes the educator. When the "you" is the student, the focus will be on gathering information about the student as a person and a learner. When the "you" is the educator, the focus will be on acknowledging our professional knowledge and stretching the boundaries of what we do.

Know speaks of professional knowledge. In this book, the "know" will be focused on using what we know about good teaching and learning. From this foundation, we consider new directions for instructional techniques and strategies to re-engage disengaged students.

Chapter 2	What	*What* Can We Learn about Disengagement? • what research tells us about disengagement • qualitative and quantitative assessment • using assessment to understand disengagement
Chapter 3	Do	What Students Can *Do* • focusing on evidence of what students have under control • gathering information and keeping records of observations and assessment • reviewing observation notes with colleagues • sharing with the student
Chapter 4	You	Getting to Know the Student as a *You* • relationship-building between teacher and student • whole-class conversations • getting to know the students' families • one-on-one conversations
Chapter 5	Know	Using What We *Know* about Re-engaging Students • considering how students think and learn to create instruction • finding instruction that moves the student forward • developing lessons with a focus on different ways of thinking • re-engaging with reading • re-engaging with writing • planning next-steps instruction

The question "What do you know?" is the heartbeat of this book, and the individual words of the question are used to enter each chapter. We'll discuss how to rethink our practice, examine what's working well, decide where we're going, and embrace the challenges—all from the perspective of what we know. It's not easy, but rising to the challenges of our everyday practice is what defines the profession of teaching and it's what makes the profession of teaching so rewarding.

The process begins with collegial conversations about the issues related to disengaged students. These conversations can be live or virtual. They can be as casual as "in the hall" comments to a neighboring teacher. They can be written and oral responses to our professional reading, or participation in educational conferences. Many educators are also involved in a wide range of qualitative or quantitative research projects that focus on the topic of student disengagement. These conversations and research have spawned terms such as "the achievement gap," "the fourth-grade slump," "the gender gap," and "students at risk." These terms have brought of issue of student disengagement into the collective consciousness.

Engaging Memories

And now that the issue of disengagement has gained a foothold in the collective consciousness, it's our responsibility to do something about it. That begins with reflecting on and sharing what we know about our own school experiences with those of our students and colleagues.

For most of us, memories of our school years run the gamut from the best ever to the worst ever. Depending on the time, place, and event, these memories can evoke feelings of excitement, triumph, wonder, concern, frustration, or despair. It's interesting to note that, when we start sharing our school years memories, they are surprisingly similar. It seems that, regardless of location, year, or even decade, our best-ever or worst-ever memories have common elements. While the names, the faces, and possibly the color on the classroom walls might differ, the situations and feelings surrounding those memories are surprisingly similar. Many are connected to times of engagement, disengagement, or re-engagement.

Let's begin with a story of re-engagement: My husband Tom, an avid hockey player since the age of three, decided early in his school career that reading served no purpose in his life and therefore wasn't worth the effort. He ignored the books carefully chosen by his mother and disengaged from any lesson or activity that involved reading. Tom's Grade 2 teacher noticed his lack of progress and scheduled Tom to attend the after-school extra support class for reading. Although Tom made what he felt was a reasonable argument, which was that hockey players don't need to know how to read, Tom's mom and his teacher insisted that he attend. As he reluctantly walked through the classroom door to begin his first extra-help session, he was pleasantly surprised to see many members of his hockey team sitting there. This, he thought, might not be so bad after all! He still had no reason to engage in reading, but at least the company could make it fun.

The extra-help reading lessons of that era were focused on sight words and phonics. The lessons provided Tom with some sense that letters played a major role in his task of figuring out words and that, once figured out, the words worked together to make some sort of story. But the rules and exceptions to the rules caused him no end of confusion. Every attempt at a new word was met with a new explanation about how the combination of letters created changes to the sounds the letters made. In short, progress was ploddingly slow and the possibility of moving beyond figuring out the words and into understanding the story seemed far away. As a result, reading continued to mystify Tom and he could see no reason to pursue the task. His attention turned to discovering new ways to amuse the others in his class and to avoid anything related to reading. At this point, Tom's experience was a classic case of disengagement.

And then Tom started collecting hockey cards. Tom's memory of his experience with his prized Jean Belliveau hockey card stands out as a pivotal moment in his learning to read. As he looked at Belliveau's name, he realized that little other than the consonants was decodable. Based on what he'd been taught, the name Jean should be pronounced "Jeen" and Belliveau should be "Bell-i-v-ee-uh." But he knew that wasn't correct, because he had heard the correct pronunciation of Belliveau's name many times. And *that* was the necessary information Tom needed. Knowing the correct pronunciation of Belliveau's name gave Tom the insight that the letter sounds he'd been taught weren't always "right."

Suddenly, Tom was aware that there was flexibility in our language and that it was up to the reader to learn how and when to use the lessons about reading that best suited the situation. As Tom proceeded to read the rest of the information on the hockey card, he connected his knowledge of sounding out with his background knowledge about hockey. He happily realized that, by combining sounding out with meaning, he "just knew" a lot of the words, the trickier ones needed some extra thinking, and some were simply unknown—and he began to feel comfortable about asking for help with those last ones.

Tom now had a purpose for reading and he re-engaged. Through reading, he could learn more about his hockey hero, his hero's team, and the entire National Hockey League. And that purpose, reading for a particular type of information, served him well for many years. It was much later, when he decided to become a teacher, that the world of reading about a wide range of topics in a wide range of genres became a part of Tom's daily life. And luckily, his own experience as a disengaged student allowed him to connect with his students in a way that served him well throughout his teaching career.

Actor and author Phil Daniels (2010) reflected on his school experiences with these words:

> I didn't like school. My mind wasn't on it. I didn't like maths—neither did we have very good maths teachers. I liked things like social studies and geography. I liked history, but all that war history seemed a bit of a lie. So in class, I talked and played truant quite a bit.

Daniels goes on to talk about discovering a drama class, and how the class and the drama educator provided for him what school didn't. Of the class, Daniels writes: "It brought out my artistic side instead of my negative side, which at school was fighting and being tough." Of his educator he said, "She was interested in you as a person, not just as a pupil."

Daniels's description of his reaction to the schooling process matches that of many students who become disengaged—his mind simply wasn't on it. The fact that one educator made such a difference, and how she made such a difference, is another common element in stories where students become re-engaged. It seems that the two key elements of re-engagement are a connection with the topic of study and a educator who responds to the student as a person and not just as a pupil.

Key elements of re-engagement:
- student's connection with the topic
- teacher who responds to the student as an individual

How Students Disengage

The next example comes from my personal experience. It further illustrates Daniels' point about the importance of the educator responding to the student as a person, and not just as a pupil. It also illustrates that, under certain circumstances, we all experience times of disengagement.

During the autumn of my Grade 3 year, the focus of our language arts class was poetry. My teacher read poems to us, we read poems in chorus, we read poems silently, we illustrated poems, we learned about the lives of the authors of the poems. We noted rhyming patterns—I even remember tapping the beats of poems on my desk. Poems were everywhere, and we were all quite excited. Then the inevitable happened—we were given an assignment to write our own poem.

And we weren't to write just any poem: our submissions would be entered in a local poetry contest. Despite my enthusiasm for what poetry had to offer, I remember approaching this assignment with very little confidence.

Write a poem? I thought. *About what??*

Completely at a loss for a topic, I did what many students who are starting to disengage from a lesson do—I stared out the window. There I sat, staring at the autumn leaves, my mind traveling far beyond the walls of the classroom to places unknown, adventures not yet experienced. But my teacher's voice ended my flight of fancy.

"Beth, don't you think you should start writing?"

I was stumped. I remembered the poems we had read, listened to, counted the beats of, and illustrated, but I had no idea of how to connect those experiences to the writing of poetry. For fifteen minutes, I busied myself with what I did know how to do—I wrote and designed the title page:

Next, I drew on my memory of poetry. I found that the memory was mostly a visual image of what a poem "looked like." My memory focused (quite conveniently, I might add) on poems that were short, with just a few words on each line. Then I searched for what else I knew. Rhyming words that make pictures… how hard could it be? I drew my inspiration from the view out the window and, to my relief, the first four lines came easily.

> The leaves fall in September
> The leaves fall smooth and fine
> Some are red
> Some are yellow

So far, so good. The rhyming part was posing a bit of a problem. "September" and "yellow" didn't seem very easy to find rhymes for, so I settled on finding a rhyme for "red" or "fine." I searched through the alphabet for a variety of possibilities. Starting with rhymes for *red*, I came up with *said, dead, fed, head*. But none of these words seemed to have anything to do with where my poem was headed. My search for a rhyme for *fine* led to *pine, spine, tine*, and *wine*. That was it—some of the leaves *were* wine-colored! The last line of my poem flowed out of my pencil.

The Leaves
by Beth Critchley
Age 8

The leaves fall in September
The leaves fall smooth and fine
Some are red
Some are yellow
And some are the colour of wine

I decided I should quit while I was ahead. It would be a short poem. I handed in my poem and awaited my teacher's comments about my newfound talent and her newfound poet.

The next day, my teacher handed back our poems. Mine was covered in comments—red ink comments about my teacher's disappointment in the short length of the poem, the odd number of beats in each line, and the lack of true poetic form. As a summary comment, she said that she was surprised that one of her best students had handed in such a disappointing poem. She wrote that I should try harder, fix it up, and hand it in again.

I considered my teacher's comments about form and beats. I didn't know what she was talking about. I loved my poem, but my teacher obviously didn't, and I didn't know why. I also knew that she expected me to try harder and do better.

But, try as I might, my rewritings couldn't top my original. I simply didn't know what to do. All I knew was that I couldn't write poetry. So I made the corrections I felt able to make—I used the left-leaning style of writing (backslanted writing was considered very cool among my eight-year-old peers) and handed it in again. My teacher called me to her desk and explained that these poems were going to be submitted in a poetry contest and so I should really do my best. What she didn't realize was that I had done my best. I didn't know how to do any better.

After much deliberation, I came to two important realizations. This is where I first experienced feelings of disengagement from school.

My first realization was that my teacher must be wrong and, more significantly, that poetry was stupid. (Since then, I've heard these words from many students—in some cases, I was the teacher and the "stupid" was one of my classroom activities.) But I knew that I had to do something, so I resubmitted the same poem in my best left-leaning handwriting, and, to make it extra special, I used peacock blue ink (a *very* cool color, back in 1963). My teacher looked at my poem and shook her head. At that moment, I remember feeling a loss of connection with her. A loss of connection with a teacher is a major step on the road to disengagement.

Late the next week, our poems lined the walls of the gym. Mine—easily identified by the color of the ink, the huge amount of white space a five-line poem left on a sheet of 8.5" x 14" foolscap, and the odd, tipped posture of those trying to read my left-slanted writing—was in the centre of the far gym wall.

The Leaves
By Beth Critchley

The leaves fall in September
The leaves fall smooth and fine
Some are red
Some are yellow
And some are the colour of wine

Beth, do you think it's
appropriate for a girl
your age to write
about wine?

From a distance, I could see that my teacher had written something at the bottom of the page. As I came near, I read her words:

Beth, do you think it's appropriate for a girl your age to write about wine?

Her comment hurt. I could feel my face flush—how embarrassing! I wanted to erase her comments and leave the judging of my poem to the parents, students, and "distinguished community members" who were visiting the poetry display. But she had written her comment in pen! The comments were now a part of my poem—and would be forever.

I know you're wondering how the writing competition turned out (and even if you're not, I'll tell you). When all was said and done, I received an honorable mention. Did I feel vindicated? Yes, but only for a very short 30 seconds. It took just that long for me to notice that every student who didn't place first, second, or third received an honorable mention. Mine was simply one poem among the masses. I had no idea if the poem had any merit at all.

And that was that. I disengaged. I shelved poetry.

But I must take a moment to interrupt this narrative of my personal crisis and offer a word of caution. The danger of sharing personal reflections about our "scarring" school experiences is that the teacher involved always comes off as the bad guy, wielding his or her red pen to totally destroy a young student's self-image and any aspirations of future success. But all my other memories of my Grade 3 teacher are positive. She was kind and caring. And although she taught me a lot about all sorts of things, there was something about the poetry unit that caused me to turn away from that sort of writing.

Looking back at this experience through the eyes of an educator reveals that it was my teacher's perception about me as a pupil that made the difference. My Grade 3 teacher had a perception of me as a good pupil. This perception was most likely based on the fact that, up until this point, I had been an enthusiastic learner of most subjects and an avid writer of short stories. Poetry, however, proved to be a different matter. My inability to match my previous accomplishments in writing challenged her perception of me as a good pupil. And, rather than providing me with the information I needed to improve my poem, she assumed that I had the information within me and I simply was not trying hard enough. With a little more effort on my part, she thought, my poetry writing would improve.

But there's the rub: improvement takes more than a little extra effort, it takes more knowledge. Without that extra bit of knowledge, I didn't know what "trying harder" involved or how to do go about expending that effort. That's what I needed the teacher for.

Lucky for me, poetry was the only element of my language arts learning from which I disengaged, because that experience was difficult enough. Imagine the disengagement that many of our students experience in subject after subject, day after day, year after year.

My experience with poetry is a mirror image of Daniels' experience with drama. Where Daniels had a teacher who responded to him as person and not just a pupil, my teacher responded to me as a pupil and not a person. And, where Daniels found a reason to re-engage, I found a reason to disengage.

So, if the key elements of the vignettes about re-engagement are a student's connection with the topic and a teacher who responds to the student as an individual, the key elements of disengagement are

- a student who experiences a loss of connection with the content
- a teacher who loses a level or some levels of connection with the student

It's important to note that disengagement is not a reflection of a student's lack of ability. It's not that disengaged students can't achieve; it's that they don't achieve. Our task is to determine why this is so. One way to accomplish this is to revisit key moments in our own educational experiences, so we can connect at some level with our students as they experience times of engagement, make every effort to reconnect during times of disengagement, and share in the times of re-engagement so that the re-engagement is sustained. That revisiting of experiences spurs us to continually re-examine our practice, know when it's time to try something new, view all options as possibilities, and choose an option for each student that builds on the answer to the question, *What do you know about students who are disengaged?*

2 *What* Can We Learn about Disengagement?

Many years have passed since I was in Grade 3—more than I care to admit. During those years, I grew up, became a teacher, and participated in hundreds of hours of professional-development sessions, graduate-level study, and research projects, each aimed at making me a better educator. Through these experiences, I was exposed to wonderful new ways of thinking, some wonderful old ways of thinking, lots of "what to do" ideas and activities that would engage my students, and a sense of excitement about implementing everything I learned. I found that most of what I learned worked well. The ideas and activities engaged most of the students, and led most of my students to the next step of their learning.

The key word in the last sentence is "most." While most of my students were engaged, and most of my students went forward on their journey of learning, it was never *all* of my students. Throughout my career, I always wondered why, despite my best efforts, there were some students who just didn't connect with the classroom experiences. These students seemed to feel the same feelings of frustration that I did in my Grade 3 poetry writing class, but for extended periods of time. As a result, they became less and less engaged in school and what it had to offer each year. It wasn't that they *couldn't* engage with the work; the problem was that they simply *weren't* engaging with the work.

In spite of their disengagement, many of these students somehow got by, but the fact that they managed to pass on to the next grade seemed to signal more of a "going through the motions" of school than an active involvement in the process. By the end of June, whether their final marks were A, B, C, or D, the final report was—for them and for me—more of a "whew" moment than a "bravo" moment.

The more I saw these students, the more I knew it was time to do something, It was time to turn "*aren't* engaged" into "*are* engaging," and to replace the *whew* moment with a *bravo* moment. As always, I turned to my colleagues for help.

The Search for Information

At that time, and throughout the years, my colleagues and I had many conversations and did a lot of reading about disengaged students. The ever-present dilemma was that, in spite of the outward signs of disengagement, we had a sense that these students had all sorts of unexposed ability and untapped potential. These students had knowledge about a wide range of topics; they had talents that provided them with hours of out-of-school discussion and activity. The problem was that their knowledge didn't match the sorts of knowledge that were expected during the school day and their talents had no outlet for expression.

My colleagues and I searched for information about how to identify and expose the ability of these students, to tap into their potential, and to find ways to re-engage them in the activities of the school day. Through our research and conversations, we soon learned that our questions echoed the questions and concerns of many educators, administrators, and researchers; we became familiar with national and international research about school improvement and educational change.

This research includes the formal and informal writing of educators, psychologists, sociologists, and medical practitioners. The content of this research is wide and varied in its scope, in the questions it asks, and in the advice it offers. Most of the research uses a common source of information about the trends and patterns of disengaged students—the published results of qualitative or quantitative assessments and surveys that are administered at a classroom, school, school board, provincial, or national level. The research on school improvement and educational change reviews this information, and then provides hypotheses to explain the results, a possible direction and goal for educational change, and suggestions for how to achieve that change. To make best use of the research, it's important for the educator to understand the data on which it rests.

The assessments and surveys that are commonly used in qualitative and quantitative research are used to inform discussions about school improvement and educational change:

- Classroom assessments provide the educator with on-the-spot information about individual student progress. Examples are reading records, writing samples, assignments, tests, quizzes, and anecdotal notes about classroom participation and performance.
- Common assessments, such as those developed and administered by educators working together at a school board or school level, provide the educational community with information about group and individual progress. For example, a school community might decide that information about progress in mathematics is important. Educational partners work together to create a common assessment of mathematics that reflects regional outcomes or standards, to administer the assessment according to established guidelines for fairness, and to review the results in a collaborative setting.
- Provincial or state assessments provide information about individual progress, or the progress of a cohort of students, at various stages throughout a student's school career. For example, Nova Scotia administers literacy and mathematics assessments at regular intervals. Results are provided at an individual, school board, and provincial level.
- National assessments provide jurisdictional and national information about the progress of students in a particular subject at a particular grade. For example, the Pan Canadian Assessment Program (PCAP) provides information about Canadian students in Grade 8.
- International assessments provide information about the performance of students relative to students in other countries. For example, PIRLS (Progress in International Reading Literacy Studies), PISA (Programme for International Student assessment), and TIMSS (Trends in International Mathematics and Science Study), provide information to participating OECD (Organisation for Economic Co-operation and Development) countries.

The research on school improvement and educational change uses survey information and assessment data to identify patterns and trends of academic success in international, national, provincial/state, and local jurisdictions as well as areas of concern, such as patterns and trends of disengagement.

The Principles for Fair Student Assessment Practices in Canada provides educators with an online reference that reviews issues of fairness, validity, and reliability in assessment practices.

Many assessments also include surveys that ask questions about parental involvement in learning and the student's attitude to specific subject areas.

An understanding of the design, purpose, and administrative procedures of assessments and surveys provides educators with an additional set of tools to understand the research about disengaged students. These tools allow us to confirm or challenge what we know and what we've read about trends in performance, who is engaged, who is disengaged, and why that is so.

But there are some cautions.

Concerns about Assessments

Before entering into a discussion about the concerns related to assessment, it's important to acknowledge that assessment is a controversial topic. Depending on one's point of view, conversations about assessment can lead to attacks on some or all forms of assessment, or defenses of some or all forms of assessment. The controversy revolves around assessment bias, issues of social justice, and misuse of assessment results for political gain. This controversy is healthy. It leads to questions that encourage the developers of assessments and users of assessments to continually improve their practice. This improvement leads to better-designed, better-administered, and better-interpreted assessments, as well as improved use of their results. Assessments and surveys have the potential to provide information to stakeholders about overall student or group performance, as well as any number of subsets of information. But—and this is huge *but*—it's important to acknowledge the concerns that accompany the misinterpretation or misuse of assessment information.

The Rationalizing of Results

When viewed quickly and through the lens of preconceived notions, there's a concern that results of assessments lead to a "first-glance" interpretation that a student's community, socioeconomic status, or gender is the "reason" for the results for that student or group of students. For example, statements like the following are often heard or read during a review of assessment data:

"Well, he's a boy, and we know that boys just don't like to write."
"Girls are better readers than boys."
"Students from that area are traditionally weak."
"Students from that country always do well."
"That community doesn't value education."
"That community is so busy taking their kids to soccer, ballet, and tennis lessons that they've no time left to just sit and read with their kids."
"His parents don't care."
"They just moved in from _____ . Those students are always weak."
"What can you expect? That family has always been like that and they've always had difficulty keeping up."

Each of these statements rationalize assessment results: they provide the speaker with a "reason," no matter how stereotypical or misinformed, for the student's results. Worse than the inaccuracy of this kind of first-glance thinking is the fact that it runs the risk of placing blame on the student's background, community, race, ethnicity, socioeconomic status, or gender. As educators, we know that first-glance interpretations and blame lead us nowhere.

An interesting corollary is that, while lack of success is often attributed to background, community, race, ethnicity, socioeconomic status, or gender, the reverse is also true. Statements about positive performance often attribute success to these factors as well. We need to challenge that attribution. I think we might not be giving enough credit to teachers for what they can do or the difference they can make.

The Deficit Perspective

The next concern about assessment is the perspective through which results are reported by the media. While assessment data might show evidence of a need to rethink some of our practices, the media headlines that accompany the release of results take us backward and not forward. How often do we read headlines like these?

Students At Risk Continue to Fall Behind
Gender Gap Continues to Widen
Community Questions Lack of Academic Growth

Such headlines serve only to create perceptions of students based on the deficit and their lack of progress in school. While it is true that we need to be aware when students are not experiencing success, and we need to acknowledge that change is needed, I'm not sure that the leading with a deficit statement is the place to start. I think we can change that start point. Stay tuned.

The Seductive Nature of Numbers

Assessment results are often presented as numbers and charts, and we all know the incredible power of numbers and charts. Numbers represent a defined quantity and something that the quantity represents. It's the "if this, then that" comfort of numbers. For example, if we're told that the temperature at a ski hill was -10° C, then we know the skiers found it very cold. If a distance between towns was reported as 100 kilometres, then we know it took an hour to drive to that town. Numbers seem so easy and clean. What we forget is that there is always information behind the numbers. For example, -10° C may be "very cold" when you consider exposure to bare skin, but not actively skiing down a sunny, windless mountain slope. Taking an hour to drive 100 kilometres presupposes a speed limit of 100 km/h, but what if the speed limit is 120 km/h? What if it's 60 km/h?

So we have to think carefully about the meaning of numbers and how we interpret the charts and graphs of research data. For example, an assessment results chart that illustrates 80% of students meeting a level of proficiency might be greeted with a round of applause. Unless we consider other factors—such as how proficiency is defined, the results of the previous year, or the number of students participating in the assessment—we're not really sure it's a round of applause or a groan of defeat that's warranted. Questions about the design, the administration, the scoring of the assessment, and how proficiency is defined are just as important as the results. Without answers to these questions, we do a disservice to the students, to the data, and to the research about the data as well.

The Political Use of Assessment Data

When assessment results are published, the media often report the data with a focus on identifying the best and worst schools, the best and worst provinces, the best and worst countries. This serves little purpose, other than enhancing the real-estate market in the areas reported as having the best schools and maintaining the depressed value of property near schools identified as worst. The actual identification of a "good school" takes much more analysis than one assessment can provide. There are untold stories of excellent schools that, through the public's single focus on assessment data, go unnoticed. The same is true for schools that are actually not functioning well but, because of an overemphasis on teaching the sorts of tasks represented on tests, might be achieving high assessment scores.

The Medical Model

A colleague of mine is a medical doctor, and is involved in the connections between educational research and medical research. This colleague cautions that educational assessment results are sometimes reviewed in the same way as the results of medical tests. Medical tests are administered to determine what's wrong with a person; once the illness or condition is discovered, the medical community responds with a cure. If applied to disengaged students, this model carries a message that disengaged students have something wrong with them. This is perhaps the most dangerous use of assessment data. It focuses our efforts on finding ways to help or fix the student, while missing the crucial point that disengagement is a student's response to schooling, not the student's response to learning. We are wired to learn, but we're not all wired to be schooled.

The Idea that Tests Reflect Performance

Assessment data in the form of test results are frequently viewed as the sole source of reliable and valid information about student performance. This is a misunderstanding of the term *assessment*. When assessment practices are understood and used to best advantage, we realize that there are many sources of information about student progress. All of our daily conversations, activities, assignments, and tests provide us with invaluable information about student progress. It's important to review this information alongside assessment data and allow each source to inform the other.

A person has the right to agree or disagree with the use of assessments, as long as that person's point of view is informed by a wide range of educational and assessment research that addresses bias, social justice, and political will.

In short, it's up to the educator to search for the information about the purpose, design, administration, scoring, and use of assessment results. One of these sources is the Principles for Fair Student Assessment Practices for Education in Canada. This document contains a set of principles that are generally accepted as indicative of fair classroom assessment practice (tests, assignments, other evaluative tools) and fair external assessment practice (jurisdictional, national, and international assessments). The use of any type of assessments and the resulting data depend on informed professional judgment.

Once we know how to interpret the information from assessments, we can use it to make a difference to our students and to our practice. The trends and patterns revealed in the assessment can provide us with information and how to use that information. It's up to educators to challenge those who use the information to make broad and often uninformed statements about our students, our schools, and our school communities; it's also up to us to continually question our practice and embrace possibilities for change. That change occurs at the school, and that's the change that has the potential to re-engage the disengaged student.

Using Assessment Information Effectively

"The power of data," my colleague Jim Rice told me, "is in the questions it provokes." From questioning comes thinking, and from thinking comes solutions. Assessment data from classroom, school, jurisdictional, and national sources provides us with the starting point for our questions. Our questions direct our thinking, and our thinking leads to solutions about how to re-engage our disengaged students.

As we formulate our questions, it's important to examine our perspective. If we're searching for information that verifies preconceived notions about the student's family, community, or gender, we need to acknowledge that this is a misinformed and unethical practice. If we ask questions that lead us to quantify negative behaviors (rates of absenteeism, occurrences of belligerence, percentage of drop outs), our focus is on the deficit and what's wrong. I don't think I'm naïve to feel that there's too much potential in our students to let a negative perspective be the entry point into our discussion. I'm proposing that we rethink our perspective, and instead ask questions that lead us to observe and define the conditions under which students are attending, participating, and engaging. If we are focusing on poor marks for classroom assignments and test scores, we need instead to search for information about when, where, and in what areas our students experience success. Creating effective questions is about looking for what's working and observing the conditions that encourage that success.

When viewing assessment results, the most effective question is "What do you know?" This question leads us to look for evidence of what the student can do. I can think of no better words to describe the process of searching for evidence of what a student knows than those of Marie Clay (1999):

> There must be a time when the educator stops teaching and becomes an observer, a time when he/she must drop all presuppositions about what this child is like, and when she/he listens very carefully and records very precisely what the child can do.

Clay's words describe the essence of knowing our students as people *and* as pupils. Her words speak of allowing students the opportunity to demonstrate who they are and what they know.

Clay describes the process through which we can uncover evidence of what the student can do:

1. Clay speaks of setting aside our preconceived notions about a student. This is one of the greatest challenges faced by the educator of a disengaged student or group of students. Knowledge of a student's race, ethnicity, community, gender, or previous academic experiences should never influence how we view a student's work. If we maintain the mindset of searching for information about what a student is able to do, we avoid making decisions based on biased notions.

2. Clay speaks of the importance of listening. An educator with well-developed listening skills has insight into the "do" perspective (rather than the "don't" perspective) of a student's learning, problem-solving strategies, and engagement with a lesson.

3. Recording precisely is Clay's next point. Recording allows us to make note of our observations and maintain a record that provides evidence of ongoing

change and progress. If we record with an eye to what the student can **do**, our notes capture the student's foundational understandings.

4. Clay's final two words—"can do"—provide the most important part of her message. There's nothing in the words *can do* that leads us to think of a student's progress in terms of a deficit, risk, or gap. Thinking in terms of *can do* opens the door to continued, forward-moving instruction that builds on what we've observed about the student's foundational understandings.

Let's explore each of Clay's tenets of good observation.

Drop Presuppositions

Clay speaks of the importance of observing, and dropping presuppositions. To drop presuppositions, it's important to acknowledge that we have them. Let's examine the perspective through which we observe a student's work.

Look at this image of an open book and quickly answer: In what direction are the pages facing? Are the pages facing toward you or away from you?

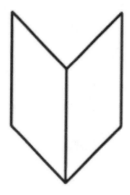

If your first glance indicated that the book is open toward you, look at the image again and shift your perspective so the pages are facing away from you. If, in your first glance, the pages were facing away from you, look at the image again so the book is open toward you. Switch back and forth between the two perspectives a few times. As you are shifting your perspective, concentrate on how the shift feels and make note of that feeling.

Let's try that again. Quickly look at the image below and answer the question: Is this an image of rabbit or a duck?

If your first glance showed you a rabbit, change your perspective so the animal's eye is looking to the left; follow the direction of the eye to the duck's bill on the left (which you first saw as the rabbit's ears). If your first glance led you to see a duck, change your perspective so the animal's eye is looking right and follow the eye to the rabbit's nose (which you first saw as the back of the duck's head.) If it's difficult to make this shift in perspective, keep trying. It's worth it to *feel* the physical sensation. That's the "aha!" moment of a shift in perspective.

You're probably questioning the relevance of this exercise and wondering what on earth this has to do with student engagement, assessment, and Clay's words about observing and dropping presuppositions. Good question! Allow me to make the connection by providing the same sort of exercise, but this time we'll look at student writing and shift our perspective from observing what the student is doing wrong to observing what the student has under control.

The student who wrote the story below was very engaged in writing, and said that she loved to write stories even though she *knew* she wasn't a good writer. Her teachers agreed, stating that, other than knowing a few sight words, this student was really a non-writer. At first glance, many would agree. As a result of spelling and spacing errors, this piece of writing is very difficult to understand.

He cht the ball ovr
hiis shodr it was prft
a prfk carh.
he mada dsktk and the
skr ws 2nte5 to ten
We one!

Note this: *2nte5*—that's exactly how "twenty-five" sounds! This is an example of a student who knows how to sound out words and will benefit from a lesson that clarifies the use of numbers and letters.

But that's a perspective based on what's wrong. Let's switch that perspective and search beyond that first glance for information about what this student has under control. To do that, we need some help to get past the spelling and spacing errors. In this case, I told the student that I was interested in knowing more about her basketball game and, while I could read some of her story easily, I needed some help with some of the words. I didn't point out the errors. I wanted to acknowledge the work she did to make her topic clear, but I also wanted to convey the message that a writer's audience must be taken into consideration. As she read me the story, I "heard," rather than "saw," the story. Here are her words:

He catched the ball over
his shoulder. It was perfect.
A perfect catch.
He made a basket and the
score was twenty-five to ten.
We won!

In this transcribed form we see the work of a student who *can* write. Remember, the ability to write is more than the ability to spell. Writing is about passing on a message to the reader. The student's message is a recount of a basketball catch that led to a win. Her story is organized in a logical sequence and her choice of words provides the reader with a clear image of the event. She has a developing sense of when to use a full stop (after *catch* and at the end of the story). She knows how to spell some high-frequency words (*a, he, we, the, it, my*) and can sound out the main consonants in most words. This is what she accomplished. This is the information on which we build. It's a much more solid foundation on which to build than a lesson that fixes what's wrong

To build on this student's story writing, a conversation with her about how she painted an image of the basketball game with her words would serve to acknowledge her message. This conversation could easily lead to a lesson about how to add more information so the plot line develops more fully. To build on the student's current knowledge of spelling, she can be taught about the purpose of standard spelling, which is to open the door of her writing for all audiences to appreciate her story. Since this student is a keen writer, she deserves to be taught some new writing strategies (right now!) and to have opportunities to demonstrate that she knows how to use each of these tools effectively. Without this instruction, this student will soon sense that her writing is "wrong" and may well become disengaged. She also needs to know that this step will take some extra time, but that the time will pay off, because more of her friends and teachers could enjoy her stories.

From a first glance about what's wrong to a more thoughtful and insightful observation of what the student has accomplished—that's the perspective shift. That's the vision through which good assessment emerges and forward-moving instructional practices evolve. It's a perspective to consider when reviewing the results of classroom assessment, common assessments, and external assessments of individual students, small groups of students, and classes of students.

Tomlinson (2007) speaks of this perspective shift and likens it to the difference between looking at the positive and negative spaces of an image:

> When I saw 'positive space' in students and reflected on them, the results were stunningly different from when I reported on 'negative space'. It gave students something to build on—a sense of possibility. I began to spend at least as much time gathering assessment information on what students *could* do as on what they couldn't.

Tomlinson's use of the words "stunningly different" could seem like hyperbole, but they're not. A perspective that switches the viewer from the traditional focus on "what not" to "what is" has the power to make significant change in how we know our students and how we plan for educational change.

Listen Effectively

To gather information about our students, it's important that we first look at how we gather that information. The key to successful information-gathering lies in what is perhaps the most important skill of effective teaching—the skill of effective listening. Effective listening provides the impetus with which we switch the perspective through which we view student work; it opens the doors to knowing the student as a person, to developing a relationship of trust, and to thinking about possibilities instead of problems.

See Assess Your Listening Skills on page 29.

We can examine our own listening skills by completing a simple survey; see page 29. As you read each question, assume that the "speaker" referred to in each question is a student, and consider your response in light of your daily interactions with that student.

The survey brings to light a variety of circumstances during which we may intentionally or unintentionally allow our preconceptions to veer us away from, override, misinterpret, or ignore the student's message. In so doing, and often without intent, we might change the student's actual message. Effective listening allows us to counter those tendencies and gather information about what the student brings to the learning situation.

Effective listening requires that we take the time to process what students are saying, reflect on their words, and then respond to those words. In today's busy classroom, allowing for even a few extra seconds of time may seem impossible. If this is the case, it's time to engage the support of our colleagues and rethink our practice to allow us more time to know our students. Since effective listening allows us to know more about our students, it's time well spent.

Record Precisely

Interpreting assessment results through the perspective of what a student has under control is good practice when reviewing the assessment results of all students. In the example on page 24, a first glance at the student's writing indicated that she "couldn't write"; a switch in perspective changed our minds. The new perspective uncovered the elements of writing she had under control and provided us with an instructional direction.

The next example illustrates the importance of not only going beyond a first glance of interpretation, but also of using assessment responsibly. The reading record shown here is a "short form" version of the original form. To the detriment of good recordkeeping, this version is becoming increasingly popular. In this version, only the student's accuracy and fluency are used to provide a measure of what the student has under control in reading.

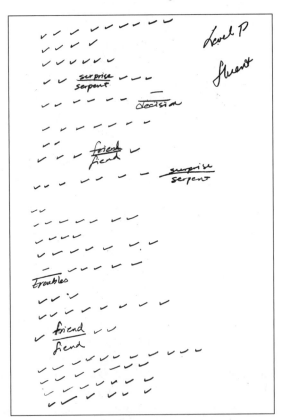

For more examples of reading records and discussion of interpreting their results, see Chapter 3.

Based on the results of this version, the student has this level of text well under control. This student's reading was accurate, fluent, and lively. The teacher indicated that she felt the student was making steady progress as he quickly worked through the levels of text difficulty. Based on these results, we would assume that the student has this level of text firmly under control and that the book was an easy read. We would be mistaken.

As we look beyond the first glance, observe carefully, and ask questions about this student's reading, we notice that the student skipped unknown words and did not correct errors. It's then our responsibility to ask the following questions:

- Did his errors maintain the meaning, grammatical structure, or graphophonic text information?
- Did he notice the errors?

If yes,

- Did he correct the errors "in his head"? OR
- Did he ignore the errors?

If the reading record had been completed according to its intended design (see Chapter 3 for a more complete discussion about the administration of a reading record), some of those questions would have been answered. A reading record includes an analysis of errors and reading behaviors, as well as a conversation with the student.

We can find the answers to the remaining questions by asking the student about the story. In this case, that's what we chose to do. In his retelling, he confidently wove a *surprise* into the narrative instead of a *serpent* (surprise/serpent), and the actions of the enemy in the story were interpreted as those of a *friend* (friend/ fiend). Since he wasn't aware of his errors, he felt very good about his retelling. This retelling makes it clear that the student recreated the plot line based on his errors.

This student deserves to be assessed in a way that provides accurate information about what he's able to do in his reading. He also deserves to know that there's more to reading than getting the words right, and to be taught how to ensure that the text makes sense and matches grammatical structures. He also deserves to learn how to notice when things go awry, how to search for information to re-establish meaning, and how to check that the search reaped meaningful results. Without that knowledge, this student may well fall into the trap that many young readers do; he reads what he can and either omits or guesses at the rest. Over time, his comprehension will suffer.

Careful observation of our youngest students as they develop as readers is essential. All too many elementary students who learn to decode accurately and quickly are assumed to have reading under control. They sound like good readers, so we assume they are good readers. But reading isn't reading without comprehension, and I'm quite convinced that the students who focus only on getting the words right are those who show up in the data on "fourth-grade slump."

The fourth-grade slump is a noted gap in achievement that becomes most evident as children transition from the learn-to-read stage to the read-to-learn stage. Students who seem to be confident readers (based on measures of accuracy and fluency) can get by with simply decoding until they are at the level of reading complexity and range of content area reading required by Grade 3 or 4. At that point, the student's reliance on "knowing the words" and patching together the meaning of the text runs counter to the development of the ability to work with all elements of the text to problem-solve and build comprehension. Students who previously experienced success in reading begin to experience difficulty and are not sure why. It must be a shock to suddenly realize that what worked well in the past no longer works, and that reading is suddenly a difficult task. This is the sort of experience that can lead a student to disengage from reading.

If we build on what this student's reading record indicates he has under control (decoding words accurately and fluently), he would profit from instruction that allows him to see reading as a problem-solving activity and to know that he has the tools to solve the problems. We start that instruction with what he knows about reading.

In a post–reading-record conversation, the teacher shared with the student her observations about his fluency and accuracy. She asked the student what he does when he comes to a tricky word. He replied, "I skip it." The teacher acknowledged skipping a word as a strategy and moved to the next step of the strategy, which was to demonstrate that when we skip a word, we don't ignore it; we keep the skipped word in our mind as we search for information to solve it. Then, we go back and see if it works. Next, the teacher provided a variety of lessons on how to do that search. She subsequently observed the child in his daily reading for evidence that he was using the information from the lessons.

A Shift in Perspective

Rethinking the perspective through which we view every student's work involves reconsidering the processes by which we gather information about the student as a person and a learner and how we interpret and use that information. It's a difficult process, because it questions what we do. But it's a good kind of difficult, because it leads us to think beyond the established boundaries of what we do and explore the possibilities of what is possible. It's this kind of difficult that makes the profession of teaching so exciting. Keeping in mind the possibilities for every child not only decreases the likelihood of student disengagement, but it also has the potential to decrease the possibility of teacher disengagement.

Assess Your Listening Skills

Answer each question with *Usually, Occasionally,* or *Seldom.* Record your thoughts and observations:

• Do you try to see the world as the speaker sees it, even when the speaker's ideas and behavior conflict with your own view of the world?

• Are you interested in the speaker as a person?

• Do you listen to the speaker willingly?

• Can you remain calm, even though the speaker is angry or excited and may be criticizing you?

• Do you give the speaker your full attention?

• Do you hear the speaker out (especially at the beginning of the conversation), even though the speaker is repetitious?

• Do you avoid jumping in and giving advice?

• When it does seem appropriate to give your observations and raise your concerns, do you raise them as questions rather than as accusations or criticisms?

• Do you not only get the main idea, but also some of the underlying feelings that might conflict with what the speaker is saying?

• Can you keep tuned in, regardless of distractions?

• Do you smile, nod, and otherwise encourage the speaker?

• Do you ask questions to be sure you understand?

• Do you refrain from pretending you understand the speaker when you don't?

• Do you check to see if you have understood the speaker?

(Adapted from Critchley, 1992)

Pembroke Publishers © 2010 *Engaging the DisEngaged* by Beth Critchley Charlton ISBN 978-1-55138-258-6

3 What Students Can *Do*

Seeing What Students Can Do

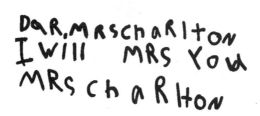

This card was made for me as I was leaving one school and moving on to another. The teacher had provided time for the students to make the cards and she had printed the correct spelling of my name on the whiteboard. Everything else was completed independently by the students.

This student's enthusiastic response to the card-making activity was unexpected. In previous writing lessons, she had done everything possible to avoid writing, including going to the washroom, breaking her pencil, and erasing with such vigor that she rubbed a hole in her paper. The teacher was delighted by the student's enthusiasm, and wondered what it was about this writing project that was so engaging to the student. That's an important question to ask the student; it's on these occasions that we find clues to re-engagement that is sustainable. The student said she really liked to do things all on her own. (I don't mind saying that I was relieved to know that her enthusiasm was not related to me leaving the school.)

The teacher made a note about this desire for independence and wondered if she had been providing this particular student too much assistance. The teacher decided that, in future lessons, she would watch for occasions when this student could take on the responsibility of completing a task alone.

At first glance (from a deficit perspective), one could say that this student has little under control: there is confusion about the use of upper- and lower-case letters; there's a misplaced comma; the spacing is haphazard; and the message is very short and very unclear.

When I was presented with the card, I was a bit mystified by the message, so I searched through the student's writing for evidence of what she could do and a possible clue to the meaning of her words.

Here's what I found: The student

- knew that a letter begins with *Dear*
- copied my name correctly
- knew that a card includes a message
- knew a comma should be somewhere in the salutation of a letter
- knew how to spell *I* and *will* and *you*
- noticed and self-corrected the misspelling of *you*

But still, the phrase "I will Mrs. you" made the message was unclear, and I decided that the next time I saw her, I would ask her to read the card to me.

When, by chance, I saw this student in the hall, she called out, "Hi, Miss Charlton," and I realized that she, like many students, was replacing the title *Mrs.* with *Miss.* The intended message of her card was, "I will *miss* you Mrs. Charlton." This chance encounter led to my most exciting observation of what this student knew how to do. (When a teacher keeps her observing eyes and ears open, even the most casual comments can reap huge benefits!) I now had evidence that she engaged in, learned from, and used a recent lesson about how to search the classroom for the spelling of an unknown word.

Here's what she did: Not knowing how to spell *miss*, she used what she learned from a lesson about how to search the classroom for an example of that word. Finding my name on the classroom wall, and thinking that it was pronounced "Miss Charlton," she copied what she thought was the word *miss*. It's a great feeling for a teacher to see that her lessons are being used!

While I was delighted she used the information from the lesson, I also acknowledged that her spelling error made a significant difference to clarity of the message. It was important to teach her how to make sure that the work she does to find the correct spelling is checked. I chatted with her about what I observed in her writing—that she noticed and self-corrected her misspelling of the word *you*, and that she searched the classroom for the spelling of a tricky word. Building on acknowledging what she did well, my next lesson provided additional information. After searching the classroom for the word, we verified that the spelling was accurate by looking for the spelling of tricky words in the context of a favorite book. This lesson provided the student with another strategy for word-solving and was much more effective than a lesson that taught her only how to spell *miss*. Knowing a wide range of strategies allows a student to move toward independence. A sense of independence leads to engagement.

In the example on page 33, the list of *can-do*s goes on and on. But just because this student is the "best writer in the class" doesn't mean we don't continue to identify what she has under control and plan a lesson that moves her forward. The search for what the student in the first sample has under control led us to a next-steps lesson; this student deserves the same consideration. Without this consideration, even a good writer can start to fade into disengagement.

When a child has a lot under control, we look for evidence of most recent learning. In this case, the student demonstrated that she had a firm grasp on inserting dialogue into a story—a very firm grasp. Based on my experience as a teacher, this overuse of dialogue is a common trend among developing writers; the ability to use quotations marks often leads a student to relay an entire story through dialogue. It's great fun for the writer, but for the reader, this stage of story writing can be confusing!

The fact that the quotation marks are not inverted on one side was a minor point I decided to deal with by mere mention; such a minor detail is probably not worth the time it takes to create a lesson.

February 10, 2004
The Surprise Package

Kim was turning nine that day and she was so excited! Suddenly there was a knock at the door. "Coming" Kim called. When Kim opened the door all she saw was a big box and two legs! "Oh my" Kim cried. "Sorry to startle you" came a muffled voice from behind the box. "Fred"? Kim asked, a little confused. Fred was the postman, and a very good friend of Kim's. "Right here" Fred said, removing the box and resting it on the step. "Who's box is that"? asked Kim. "Why, it is yours"! Fred exclaimed. Kim was to shocked to talk. "It's for your birthday" Fred said. Then Fred put on a serious face. "It is your birthday, right" He asked. "Yes, of course but I don't understand who woul' send me this big of a parcel"! Kim said finally getting her voice back. "Someone who"—Fred began but he was cut off by Kim's Mom who called "Kim"! "Come here, sweetie". "Look, I have to go Fred." "See you later". "Byyy Kim" Fred yelled as Kim disapered inside. "Look, Mom look"! Kim cried when she came into the room were her mom was. "I got a present for my birthday"! "Well, Open it already"! her mom exclaimed. So Kim sat down and started peeling off the tape from the box when she suddenly heard a little, muffled voof! "What was that"? she said quickly. "I don't know" he

Not wanting to diminish her accomplishment, I decided to introduce this student to another a genre of writing that complemented and built on what she was already doing. We moved from dialogue in stories to dialogue in script writing.

The student was delighted to transfer her knowledge of using dialogue with quotations to dialogue in script form and quickly came to realize that, while both genres allow the author to explore dialogue, she now had a choice as to which was the best genre for the story she was writing. Choice maintains engagement.

Basing Instruction on What Students Can Do

Using the Reading Record

A reading record is an oral reading assessment that uses a series of codes and anecdotal notes to inform a teacher about a student's oral reading. The codes are used to acknowledge which words are read correctly and to make note of errors and reading behaviors. Codes are interpreted through the lens of what the student is doing, and not with the lens of what the student is not doing. The anecdotal notes are written with an eye to discovering the problem-solving strategies a reader has under control and how the reader is using these strategies. When completed according to the intended design, a reading record provides a valuable record of what a student has under control in reading. It's like a window into a students' thinking about how he or she approaches reading.

Unfortunately, we often use a reading record to obtain superficial information, such as determining a student's instructional reading level based on reading accuracy and fluency level. When this happens, we are minimizing the use of a reading record and missing the wealth of information it provides. See the reading record here for an example of this.

For more information about how to complete a reading record, I suggest *Running Records for Classroom Teachers* by Marie Clay. In this short book, teachers can find all they need to know about the reading record procedures.

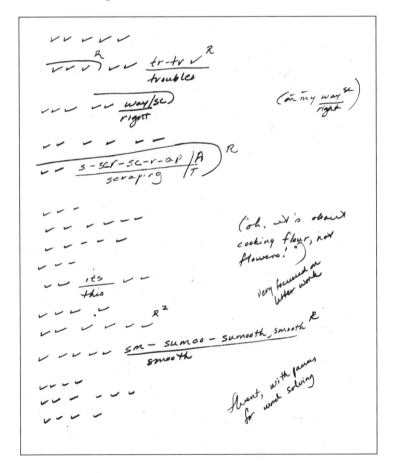

34

The reading record is not a simple tracking device to measure a child's progress up the ladder of reading levels. The power of a reading record comes when we look beyond the accuracy and fluency rating and examine what the child does with text. We ask probing questions, such as

- Does the student understand what he/she reads?
- Does the student notice his/her errors?
- If so, what does the student do when he/she makes an error?

In the reading record on page 34, the student is reading accurately and fluently. That's one piece of information, but the following teacher notes are what provide real insight into what the student can do as a reader:

- *fluency is only interrupted by problem solving*
- *used context and meaning to correct* flour/flower *(said, "Oh, I thought the story was about a flower, not the flour you bake with – it makes more sense now")*
- *sounds out tricky words*
- *nods head, smiles at appropriate places while reading*

This student's reading record provided the teacher with a lot of information about the student's comprehension of text (pausing and reviewing text that doesn't make sense; noticing the change of meaning resulting from a confusion of homonyms; and appropriate gesturing to meaningful parts of the text). The teacher also observed what the student did when she came to a tricky word: she sounded it out. The teacher used this information to plan the next lesson: he decided to commend the student's *flour/flower* correction and link that awareness to a lesson using homonyms as an example of context and meaning as a problem-solving strategy for tricky words (text passages that used homonyms to create humorous situations were used).

In the last example (on page 36), the student's reading record isn't useful. The level of text is so difficult that all the student's efforts go into working through difficult words; he has little energy left to formulate meaning. This reading record simply displays what the student can't do and leads to lessons about fixing what's wrong (but where would we even begin?). A lesson focused on fixing what is wrong is no way to re-engage a reader, so this reading record should not be used to make any instructional decisions about a child. To re-engage, a student should hear evidence of what he or she can read, and that only comes when most of the words are read correctly.

Record Keeping

As we listen to and observe what a student has under control, we need an effective way to take notes about what we see and to maintain records of those observations. At present, there are thousands of checklists, graphic organizers, and rubrics designed to facilitate record-keeping of student learning. If these work for you, enable you to make note of what the student has under control, and lead you to lessons that move the student forward rather than fixing what's wrong, then they're serving their purpose.

Quite honestly, I find many of the checklists, graphic organizers, and rubrics somewhat cumbersome. For my purposes, many are too wordy; worse yet, despite their wordiness, they never quite reflect the student as I see him or her. I end up making addenda—many addenda—to these forms. After I'm finished, what started as a beautifully designed template ends up as an unreadable mess,

✓✓✓

✓✓ _t t tn_ —
   tonight

   ✓ ✓ ✓   _w wn   w-hen_   ✓
              when

✓✓ _on_ ✓ ✓ ✓
   one

   ✓ _t_ /A ✓ ✓
     trying /T

   ✓ ✓ ✓

✓✓ ✓ ✓ ✓ _ch-r-s_ ✓
              chairs

   ✓ ✓ ✓ ✓

✓ ✓ ✓ ✓   ¯
          leaving

   ✓ ✓ ✓ _in   ing_
          matching

✓ ✓
¯   ✓ ✓
opening

✓

- looks at pictures
- looks at me
- said "This is really hard!"

} we stopped here and moved to another book

covered with margin notes, arrows, and asterisks that obliterate the words on the checklist and render it almost useless. As a result of the mess I create, the information can be understood by no one other than me. This does little to promote collegial conversations about student progress.

The Scribbler

For my purposes, the best form of record keeping is one that is simple and flexible. I use one that was provided to me by my husband, who has the gift of making complicated things seem simple. As a teacher, my husband developed the best note-taking procedure I've seen. It's called a scribbler (see picture on page 37). Each student has a two-page spread in the scribbler. Throughout the day, the teacher's notes about each student are recorded on sticky notes and placed on the student's two-page spread. When time is available, the sticky notes are organized into topics. Attach a picture of the student to the top of the two-page spread; this reinforces and maintains the focus on knowing the student as a person.

The beauty of this system is that each sticky note can be moved around easily, allowing the teacher to not only organize the comments by subject area, but also make connections between a student's "can do" in one subject area and a "can do" in other area. The manipulation of sticky notes provides the teacher with information about a variety of topics that can be used in a variety of subject areas. As the sticky notes begin to connect, the teacher can see patterns of student interests and student knowledges, and ideas about future directions and topics of lessons begin to emerge.

For those more technologically inclined, the scribbler can be used with software, such as Inspiration®, that allows quick note-taking and manipulation of the notes.

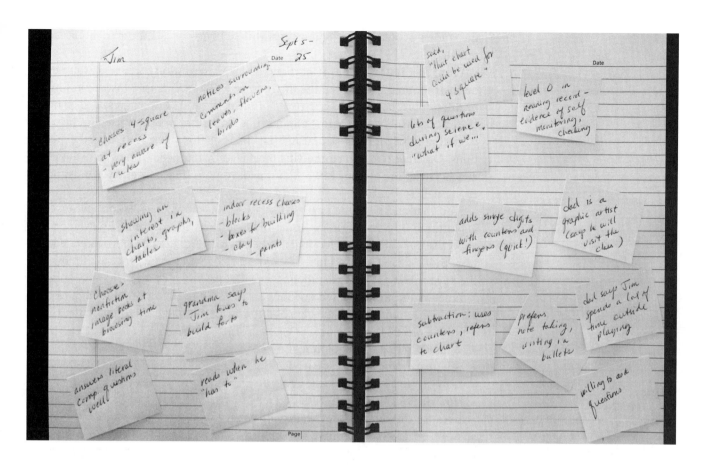

For example, a student who demonstrated an interest in travel and maps provided me with a great link from his knowledge in this area to a language arts lesson in text features. Another student who was a star soccer player and kept detailed statistics about players, teams, and leagues allowed me to transfer this knowledge to a math lesson that used these statistics to present the concepts of mean, mode, and median. Observing a student's interest in sailing provided me with a link between his knowledge of ocean currents and wave patterns to a science unit on movement and sound. More examples of how to make connections between student interests and curriculum content are found in Chapter 4.

Community Conversation

Reviewing observation notes with colleagues allows a teacher to explore new possibilities of instructional practice. A Community Conversation provides a forum for teachers to meet and review what they have observed about a student or group of students. When these conversations occur in the context of what the student can do, they are exciting and productive.

During a Community Conversation, teachers share ideas about developing different instructional approaches that are focused on re-engaging the disengaged learner. It's a discussion of exploring possibilities, extending what we know, and using that knowledge to explore new and possibly very different instructional directions. The Community Conversation presupposes professional expertise, so each possibility is explored, as long as the possibility is focused on moving the student forward from what the teacher has observed that student can do, what the student's interests are, and what additional knowledges the student has accumulated.

From that foundation, the participants in a Community Conversation decide on instructional goals, what the instruction will look like (the instruction might be different from what has been tried in the past), and how progress will be noted (the measurement of progress might differ from what has been tried in the past). Note that *different* does not mean "less than" or that there are reduced expectations. *Different* refers to connecting what is known to what is new in novel ways. Teachers explore all they know about pedagogy to find new entry points for re-engaging a student.

And that's perhaps the best part of a Community Conversation, because the exploration of possibilities shines a light on the wide range of knowledge and expertise our colleagues have. All teachers—recent graduates, mid-career educators, those close to retirement—have knowledge and experience that might be the key to re-engaging the student.

A set of questions—based on Cooperider, Lord & Hammond (2008) and conversations with my colleague Gordon Johnson—can be used to guide the Community Conversation:

- What does this student know?
- Where can this knowledge lead?
- How do we get there?
- How do we know when we've arrived?

Because these questions begin with what the student knows, the search for answers begins on a positive note and the conversation is focused on forward movement. The answers are not about fixing, they're about acknowledging what has been accomplished, exploring what is possible, and deciding the most engaging way to scaffold between the accomplished and the possible.

Sharing with the Student

Our observations and Community Conversation are not complete until we include the student. For example, the educator should feel comfortable reviewing the information on the scribbler sticky notes with a student, because it allows a student to see what's been accomplished, how his or her interests and knowledges are valued, and how this information leads to future lessons. This sharing is a clear demonstration of the teacher's interest in the student. When a student has the chance to see how sticky notes have moved from an area of interest to a subject specific lesson, that student sees the answer to the most common questions of the disengaged student: "What is the point of this?" and "How will I ever use this information?"

Once you have collected the information about your students, it's easy to start noticing the trends and patterns of interests and knowledges about the students in your class. This makes instructional planning for small groups and larger groups much easier.

Student input, as to whether or not the student feels this is a fair representation of what he or she knows, should be a part of the teacher–student conversation. This element of the Community Conversation demonstrates that the teacher values what the student brings to the learning situation and provides an opportunity to establish trust between teacher and student. This trust leads to re-engagment.

Planning Instruction

As we gather information about what a student knows and use it to plan the next steps of instruction; we remember that learning is expected and ongoing progress must be noted. I mention this now because I've spoken a lot about searching for information about what a student can do. There are two possible misconceptions associated with this message.

Some may feel that the search what for a student has under control is tantamount to viewing the world through rose-colored glasses: that what we are saying is that all kids will be fine, we should simply let them develop at their own rate. That's not the intended message; in fact, nothing could be further from the truth. Determining what a student is able to do and building on that knowledge is actually about using the information to record the student's foundation, or what the student knows right now. From that point, we plan lessons with high expectations and continuous monitoring for ongoing progress.

There is also a common misunderstanding that determining what a student is able to do is the same as determining the student's strengths. I disagree with this message and think that the process of searching for strengths, as we often define it, is misguided. Here's why.

As educators, it's common to hear discussions about using our observations and assessment data to identify each student's areas of strength and then using those strengths to address the student's needs or weaknesses. The phrases "build on a student's strengths" and "helping a student address needs or weaknesses by building on strengths" are the mantra of many involved in finding answers to the questions of disengagement. While these discussions are beneficent in intent, I think they lead us astray. Look at the evidence: after years of using this model, we still have too many students who are disengaged from the schooling process. Perhaps it's the mindset these words create that needs to be examined. While the mindset has merit in its intent, the actual practice should provoke questions.

Defining Terms

I think the problem comes from our interpretation of the words "strengths," "needs," and "helping." Some might see a discussion about strengths, needs, and helping as purely a matter of semantics. That's probably true. But the interesting thing about exploring matters of semantics is that we are forced to explore the multiple meanings, uses, and power of words and how those words inform how we teach. That's what rethinking our practice is all about.

"Strengths"

In educational discourse, we identify a student's strengths by the ability to complete a task successfully. For example, a student who completes a visual arts assignment well is considered to have a strength in the visual arts. A student who reads and responds well is considered to have a strength in reading. A student who writes a good story is considered to have a strength in story writing. But we have to question if these are actually strengths. The concept of strength is associated with power, intensity, and excellence, and I'm not sure that completing something well is actually a strength. Perhaps the student's demonstration of work is strong relative to other subjects; however, if that's what we mean, we should be more accurate in our description. We should reserve the word *strength* for occasions when there is evidence that the student has demonstrated knowledge, skill, and mental or physical ability that truly exceeds the expectations of the age group.

The danger of misusing the word *strength* is that it allows us to make to the mistaken assumption that all is well. This complacency could lead to three counterproductive situations:

1. It could lead the student or the parent to believe that this level of accomplishment is all that's necessary.
2. If we use the word *strengths* to build a student's confidence, it simply doesn't work. Students see through this ruse. As a result, the student loses trust in us, and our words do not actually lead the student to increased motivation.
3. If, by relaxing our instructional focus in the area defined as a strength, we expend more effort on the student's "needs," we limit opportunities for students to extend learning in areas of interest and success.

None of these lead to a student's full development as a learner.

"Needs"

The use of *needs* has also veered away from its dictionary definition. Needs, in educational discourse, has become associated with academic weakness. This association with weakness leads us to negative words and phrases, such as "problem," "lack of ability," "failing," "lack of power," or "lack of determination." These words all speak of something being academically or behaviorally wrong, and lead to imperatives for the educator to help or fix what's wrong.

This interpretation of the word *needs* can lead to three counterproductive situations:

1. When we focus instruction on areas where a student experiences difficulty, the student enters each lesson knowing it will be "hard"—not the best way to re-engage a student.
2. By teaching specific lessons addressed at specific "need," we focus on teaching the unknown rather than building on what is known. Lessons that focus on what isn't known are gap-filling lessons; the problem is, we don't know how deep the gap is. Unless a lesson is situated on or connected to information or strategies the student has under control, the topic of the lesson may become an unattached item of information.
3. When we focus on what the student doesn't have under control, the student learns to anticipate the beginning of each lesson as one more confirmation that lessons have little application to what he or she knows or has a purpose for. What's engaging about that?

"Help"

As teachers, our role is provide instruction that acknowledges what the student can do and provide the strategies to move the student forward. That sort of teaching is scaffolding, not helping. Scaffolding is powerful; it builds on what is known and results in lessons that provide the students with just the right amount of challenge. "Help" sends the message that the child needs assistance to complete the task; this perspective diminishes the opportunity for a student to apply the lesson's strategies at a level of independence.

Using the word *help* this way leads to three counterproductive situations:

1. The role of the teacher is perceived by the student as that of a helper, someone to act as a shield against challenge. For the student, the distinction between rising to a challenge and giving in to the idea that a challenge is too difficult

becomes blurred. The student misses opportunities to experience the success that comes with effective problem-solving.

2. A teacher who sees his or her role as that of a helper views the student as less than capable; i.e., as needing help. This is reflected in lesson planning that focuses on making up for the perceived deficiencies in the student's learning, rather than lessons that build on the student's capability.

3. In an effort to help, we all too often provide compensatory practices: e.g., reading to a student instead of providing text at an instructional level; or letting a student who finds spelling difficult dictate stories to a scribe instead of providing instruction to build on what the student knows about spelling.

To avoid the interpretation of teaching as "helping," begin the lesson-planning process by thinking first about where the lesson will take the student, and how close to independence that is. When we can step back and observe a student completing the tasks of the lesson or applying the information from the lesson without ongoing prompts or clues, we know we've led that student to independence. That allows the student to experience what success feels like. It also allows the teacher to share in that success. That's engaging for all.

4 Getting to Know the Student as a *You*

When building any relationship, one person gathers information about another person. The relationship has a better chance of success if the information is focused on the positive. It's about observing the "can do"s, not the "can't do"s, and it's about seeing the "you" in the person. Knowing the "you" allows trust to develop. A positive and trusting teacher–student relationship is the ticket to engagement and the foundation of school success.

Relationship-building takes time, but it's worth it. Think of it this way: As educators, we acknowledge that it takes time to set up classroom routines. We would never expect our students to understand and use all of the classroom routines and rules within the first few days of school. If we acknowledge the time needed to set up classroom routines, we should also acknowledge the time needed to get to know our students—to really know them. This time doesn't take away from teaching or learning; it enhances teaching by providing the educator with information about what the student brings to the learning situation, and it enhances learning by providing the student with a sense that he or she is an important part of the daily dynamic of the classroom.

The "getting to know you" ideas included in this chapter are just a few of many. These and other relationship-building activities should remain a part of our daily practice throughout the year. The primary purpose of these activities is to re-engage students; the continued use of the thinking behind these activities serves to sustain re-engagement.

Class Conversations

"The supposedly necessary elements of effective schools (such as expectations, a well-defined focus, coordination, evaluation, and curriculum) although not to be diminished, were, however, all overshadowed by schools where educators were observed to have strong interpersonal skills." (Critchley, 1992)

There's nothing better than a good conversation to get to know someone. You might view conversations as a time away from teaching, but fear not. Classroom conversations intersect easily with any part of the curriculum that includes communication and problem-solving; luckily most subjects have those elements included.

To begin, schedule time each day for a conversation. You'll want the conversation to be natural, so schedule a flexible 5 to 15 minutes that can be used when an interesting topic of conversation arises. As each day unfolds, take advantage of questions, points of interest, or a lesson–life connection to engage the students in a conversation about that topic. Some conversations will involve the whole class, some will be with small groups, and some will be with an individual student. Some conversations might last only a minute or two and some will be longer, but each provides an opportunity to connect. To ensure that these conversations are a part of each school day, write "flexible conversation time" in the margin of your plan book. At the end of the day, ask yourself, "Did I chat with my students today?"

Once you've included classroom conversations in your daily schedule, plan to monitor the teacher-talk/student-talk ratio. Often, in a desire to maintain order in the classroom, the teacher does most of the talking. We assume that talking leads to loss of control, so we limit the opportunities for students to talk. But that's an example of reacting to a situation in the negative (remember the optical illusion on page 23?). To switch that perspective, think about what students know about speaking and listening. We know that any opportunity to have a conversation about a subject of interest has the potential to engage a lot of students, so why not take advantage of this interest? Student interest is the starting point for engagement, and engagement leads to a sense of order.

For classroom conversations to be successful, the logistics of a classroom conversation need to be learned. While most students are very comfortable having conversations in social situations, they might not be aware that the rules for conversations with friends differ from the rules for classroom conversations, so instruction in how to participate in a classroom conversation might be necessary.

A lesson about classroom conversations builds on what students know about social conversations. To begin planning, observe your students during conversations with friends and bring those observations to class. For example:

- one person finishes another student's sentence
- two people look at each other, and say "I know!"
- some conversations are really loud
- some people stand close when they talk; others stand farther back
- some people include a lot of examples and say things like, "How would you feel if…?" or "It's like the time I…"
- some people have conversations while they play games; others stop the game to talk
- some conversations don't get finished at recess and you wonder if they ever do get finished
- some people are comfortable walking into an existing conversation; other people wait to be invited
- some people listen a lot and speak a little; some people speak a lot and don't listen as much

As you display your observations, invite the students to comment. The comments can be explanations of, confirmations of, or challenges to your observations. Once the students' comments are meshed with your observations, you'll have a mutually agreed-upon set of rules for social conversations. The focus of this lesson is that there are different types of conversations; no one type is better than others. The difference is related to the purpose of the conversation.

Conversation Topics

To begin, you might need to have some conversation topics on hand. When choosing a topic for your first conversations, take the lead from your students. Ask them about their interests. Use simple questions as prompts:
- If you weren't in school what would you be doing?

- If you could listen to any music (play any sport, go any place), what (where) would it be?
- If you could meet (text, Tweet, or Facebook) anyone in the world, who would it be?

Once you have the answers to these questions, keep your eyes open for information about these topics and choose topics for discussion that intersect with your students' areas of interest. Here are a couple of ideas:

- A display of a recent pop culture headlines greeting the students as they enter the room is sure to get the conversation going.
- For students who are digitally inclined, prepare an electronic display of the course content for the day with an attention-getting fact about or application of the lesson's content circulating like a "ticker" at the bottom of the page. The content of the ticker acts as a purposeful lead into the day's lesson.

May 6th Schedule

9:00 - 11:00: Language Arts
          - Media Studies

11:00 -12:00: Math

1:00 - 1:45: Physical Education

1:45 - 2:45: Science

2:45 - 3:30: Social Studies

... Studies show video games cause increased violence ... Studies show video games cause incre

We know that the idea of fame and famous people holds a lot of capital for many students, and we often assume that it's the movie stars, sports heroes, and recording artists who are of most interest. Be prepared to dig a little deeper. When I asked my students who they would most like to have a conversation with, the answers were wide-ranging and completely unexpected. Students who had formerly seemed disengaged from participation in classroom discussions grabbed hold of the invitation and offered suggestions such as Stephen Hawking, astronauts, the principal, restaurant owners, and prison guards. Some students wished it was possible to have a conversation with an endangered animal or a bird flying south.

From this one question about who they would like to talk with came a wealth of information about the students' interests. Once the question was asked, I knew a quick response was necessary. Knowing that actual conversations with these people (or animals) were unlikely, virtual conversations saved the day. By searching for links to interactive interviews, blogs, and websites, each student had an opportunity to engage with the person (or animal) of choice.

The fact that that a simple question led to engagement demonstrates that our search for ways to re-engage students doesn't mean we have to create classroom "events." Often, the simple things reap the most benefit.

The use of classroom conversations can be extended into lessons that encourage thinking beyond a literal interpretation of a person's words. Search the Internet for quotes from people of interest, post a quote, and start a conversation about it. Here are some examples:

Stephen Spielberg: I dream for a living.
Steve Nash: You should be able to voice your opinion and respect the voice of the other side.
Justin Timberlake: As time goes by people will see who I am for who I am.
Beverly Cleary: I wanted to be a ballerina. I changed my mind.

As classroom conversations evolve into a regular part of classroom routine, use the information you've gathered about student interests and group those interests by category. Review current pop-culture trends and information and create discussion topics. Use novel ways to introduce discussion topics:

- an e-mail to all students that simply states the topic of conversation

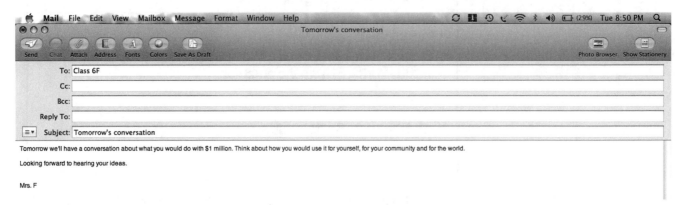

- a "Take a minute to think about . . . ." slide on the overhead, timed to appear random to the class
- a "Before we begin, let's think about…" message slipped inside the student's notebook or textbook
- an announcement from the principal to the class or to the whole school that encourages discussion about a certain topic at some time during the day. At the end of the day, teachers can come together to share the results of their class conversations. It's a terrific way to get a sense of how students throughout the school are thinking.

Make notes during your conversations about which topics were engaging to which students. To follow up on conversations and to demonstrate that you were listening to and interested in a student's words, insert a note into a student's notebook; for example

I remember that you spoke about this singer the other day, so I thought you might be interested in listening to one of her songs today—maybe as we clean up for lunch.
or
The other day, you said _____. Could you give me some more information about that?

As you plan your classroom conversations, don't steer away from controversial issues. The edgier the topic, the more involved the students. Be prepared for these conversations and be honest with the students. You may need to explain that, despite the interest, there may be limits to what is allowable within the classroom context.

Questions like these let students know you were listening to them. That's a powerful message for a student to receive.

Conversations about Discrepant Events

During my years as a resource teacher, I started many of my lessons with a simple science experiment. Watching a baking soda volcano erupt, a cork rocket launch as high as the third floor of the school, a flower turn from white to blue, a crystal form on a string, or a coffee filter turn into a rainbow of colors always engaged students and led to questions and conversations. It was a great way to start a conversation and provided a hook to the reading and writing portions of the lesson. The students' questions and conversations about the experiment led us to the content we wrote about or read about. Not only did the experiments engage students in language arts, it created a fascination with science.

My use of science to promote conversations took an interesting turn after a conversation with my colleague, Bev Williams. Bev introduced me to the concept of discrepant events, and I soon realized the power of discrepant events to spark conversation and questions among all ages of students. A discrepant event is a situation that causes the observer to be puzzled or to experience a moment of disequilibrium—it challenges what we know and what we expect. As such, a discrepant event would cause students to pause, take note, and respond with questions or hypotheses. Introducing a discrepant event is a great way to engage students.

Here's an example of teaching with a discrepant event:

- Fill a sealable plastic bag 2/3 full of water.
- Ask, "What will happen if I insert a sharpened pencil into this bag?"
- Insert a sharpened pencil into the bag.
- Invite responses.
- Ask, "What will happen if I insert another sharpened pencil into this bag?"
- Invite responses.
- Continue until six to ten sharpened pencils have pierced the bag, asking for a new prediction each time.

Are you wondering what happens? Give it a try and find out. Make note of your thinking at each stage of the process, so you have a real connection with the students as you present the experience to them.

No matter the age of your students, a discrepant event is a sure-fire way to engage them by eliciting questions, predictions, and wondering.

Classroom Dialogue

Conversations allow us to gather information about our students, develop a relationship with our students, and come to an awareness of what our students know.

Classroom dialogue is a powerful tool that exposes students to importance of asking questions, the importance of listening, and the many and varied ways of thinking about a topic. It takes the emphasis off answering a question correctly and places it on meaningful dialogue. Meaningful dialogue has a much greater chance of engaging students. It sends the message that there are many ways to be right.

Perhaps most obvious, but often overlooked, is the fact that classroom conversations, by their very nature, provide exposure to a wide range of language structures and vocabulary development. Both play an important role in the development of reading comprehension, writing, or any subject area that requires students to use language to think, question, and problem-solve (which, as we know, is true of all subject areas).

Effective Listening

For listening instruction that engages students, begin by asking them to think about the following questions before you play a sound clip about a topic of interest—a piece of music, a podcast, or a sports cast:

> *I'm going to play you a song (sound clip) by _____. As you listen, think about the following questions:*
> * *What is this song (sound clip) about?*
> * *How did you get that information from what you heard?*

After playing the song, discuss the answers to the questions and add questions that focus on the active elements of listening:

> * *How does it feel when you're really listening?*
> * *How does it feel when you know someone is listening to you?*

These questions focus the student on what listening *feels* like and how it feels to be listened to. These questions personalize the listening experience and are more effective than the traditional lesson about what good listening looks like (eyes forward, back straight, feet on the floor, mouths closed). Let's face it, how many of us do our best listening when we're sitting ramrod straight? I listen best when I'm relaxed on the couch or curled up in chair. I also know that the listening posture can hide signs of disengagement. I've had students who were sitting straight, looking forward, and seemingly engaged with my lesson… except that they had tiny ear buds in their ears. Yes, they were listening, but certainly not to me. Other students have mastered the art of looking as if they are listening, but are actually daydreaming about any number of topics.

Once the students have had the discussion about how listening feels, ask them to do a self-assessment of their own listening habits. The wording of the questions in Assess Your Listening Skills on page 29 can be adapted to all age levels and shared with students as a self-assessment of their own listening.

Use activities like the ones that follow to promote listening in the classroom.

See page 55 for an adaptation of Assess Your Listening Skills that could be used with early elementary students.

Stop Everything and Listen

I often stop my instruction by raising my hand, palm open, in a signal that means, "Stop everything and listen." This simple 30-second diversion allows students to focus on the sounds and the meaning of the sounds around them. As my hand is raised, students notice a gradual decline in classroom noise and a gradual increase in environmental sounds, both inside and outside the classroom. Once the classroom is quiet, I ask my students to listen for a very specific sound. Once the sound is identified, the students talk about how the listening experience felt. This makes listening a physical experience; as such, it seems to be more meaningful and memorable. I've found this activity allows students to develop a firm grasp on what listening really is.

When I was teaching in Bermuda, my classroom windows were always open. I frequently asked my students to stop everything and listen for a specific sound in nature. One day, I asked them to listen for the sound of a kiskadee, a very common bird in Bermuda. Once we heard the bird's call, a student said, "I hear kiskadees all the time, but I never really listened to them before. Now I realize that they change their call just a little bit. I wonder if that means anything?" That's an example of how powerful listening is—listening leads to wondering and thinking.

Listen and Watch

As we engage in conversations, we know that there's a lot more to it than saying the words and listening to the words. There are elements of body language, intonation, and gesture that add to the message. A lesson that teaches students how to interpret these elements is one of the simplest lessons I know.

Present a muted video clip to students. As they watch, demonstrate how to search for clues about the message of the clip. Turn on the sound and compare what you noticed in the muted video to the video clip with the sound on. Record students' observations.

After the discussion, ask small groups of students to prepare a script of common playground situations; e.g., a conversation between two friends, a crowd watching a soccer game, a mother encouraging her son to enter the school on the first day. Have each group film a 30-second video of their situation. Each group shares the first viewing of their video without sound, and their classmates discuss the silent messages received from the setting of the video, the scenario that unfolds, and the body language of the people in the video. The next step is to share the video with the sound on, and to listen as students talk about how the words confirm their predictions about the scenario, and how stress and intonation alter or enhance the meaning of individual words.

The Power of Questions

An important element of a conversation is the ability to ask questions. Actually, a good conversation celebrates the power of asking questions and it clears up the misunderstanding that asking a question is an indication that you don't know something. Questions that are naturally embedded in a conversation demonstrate that you do know something and you've *decided* that you want more information about that something. The use of the word "decided" is the key; it provides the student with the power to view questions as something to be used for his or her own purposes. A lesson such as I Wonder Why… provides an engaging introduction into developing and using questions effectively.

I Wonder Why…

"I Wonder Why…" questions allow students to feel the power of developing and asking questions. When you pose a question about an everyday fact or custom, students are encouraged to use their questioning to discover the history or the reason for it.

Here are some I Wonder Why questions that I've used recently at a variety of age levels. (Many more are available by simply searching *I Wonder Why* online.)

I Wonder Why…
- most pencil barrels are yellow
- most barns are painted red
- hamburgers are called that when there's no ham in them
- some sounds make us shiver

- Google is called Google
- some chefs wear tall, pleated, white hats

It's important to choose questions that build on a student's background knowledge. For example, a student with some experience with tennis may be intrigued by the question, "I wonder why a score of zero in tennis is called *love*?"; a student with no background knowledge may be less inclined to engage with this question.

This lesson begins with a think-aloud. Describe for your students the process by which you create your questions and how new questions evolve from previous questions. Use this procedure:

I Wonder Why... most pencils are yellow?
1. Think about everything you know about pencils.
   - *Pencils: wood, school, sharp, lead, long, cylinder*
2. Think about everything you know about the color yellow.
   - *Yellow: caution, color of school bus, color of gold, common color*
3. Create questions that connect pencils with the color yellow.
   - *Since school buses are yellow, is yellow a school color?*
   - *Is yellow paint the cheapest paint because yellow is such a common color?*
   - *Are pencils yellow because yellow is close to the color of wood?*

Once again, this lesson explores what the student knows and provides a link to what is new. Questions that reflect a student's areas of interest provide a way to engage the student to share his or her knowledge about that topic and learn more about that topic.

Once you've posed a few I Wonder Why questions, create a space in the classroom or on the class web page for the students to enter their own I Wonder Why questions. Involve parents by sending a Wondering question home with your students. Ask parents to think about possible answers before searching for the correct answer on the Internet or through other sources.

Questions that encourage students to wonder not only are engaging, they also provide information to educators about a student's use of cognitive strategies such as connecting, predicting, visualizing, determining importance, inferring, analyzing, and synthesizing. Observing students as they wonder provides information about how students draw on prior knowledge, then question and organize that knowledge in way that reflects a cause-and-effect relationship.

Beyond Face-to-Face

Over the years, I've heard hundreds of students say something like "Every great activity is ruined by the follow-up writing assignment." Remember that sometimes simply talking about something provides enough of an opportunity to learn and to demonstrate learning.

But there are times when writing down conversations is useful—as long as it's purposeful. For example, students can "write conversations" with classmates through their classroom library books. As a student reads a book, he or she puts "thoughts to future readers" on sticky notes throughout the book. The next reader comes across these notes, responds to them, and adds a notes for the next reader. It's like an anonymous book club, and the students I've used it with find it adds a special element to the reading.

You'll notice I haven't included the answers to the I Wonder Why questions. Although explanations are readily available through an Internet search, I suggest that you go through the process of wondering and questioning first. That will allow you to plan your own think-aloud as you ponder your possible solutions, then search for the answers to the questions. You'll find the answers are steeped in the history and the culture of many peoples.

Using the technology that is at the forefront of student-to-student communication, written conversations extend beyond the classroom and into the world. Educators who take advantage of Twitter, blogs, and social networks acknowledge a major source of engagement for today's students and use this engagement to encourage conversations with people all over the world. Rather than banning text conversations and web surfing, make them one part of classroom interaction. With the understanding that a school has stricter rules about access to topics and sites, and agreeing that some sites must be blocked, students can set up online conversations with people of note, people in the news, and people within the same classroom. The topics of these conversations and the questions asked during these conversations can provide the teacher with information about a student's interests, the types of questions a student asks, and the depth to which a student understands a topic. For example, an opportunity to interact with a favorite singer on a tour of Europe, to interact with the blog of Ed Satfford as he travels through the Amazon, to ask questions of James Raffan as he travels through the Far North, or to keep in touch with kids three rows over in the same classroom are opportunities to re-engage the student with some of the primary purposes of education—communicating, asking questions, and problem-solving.

Some educators are concerned that the conventions (spelling, grammar, etc.) of online conversations are diminishing a student's ability to use standard writing conventions. Once again, this is seeing the situation from a negative perspective. Why not acknowledge the student's interest in and use of online communication and accept this as a valid form of communication? If we have students explore the purpose and standards of text communication, it becomes clear to them that there are rules to social media communication and that the rules make communication easier. Our role is to build on this knowledge by introducing other forms of written communication and explaining the purpose of the standards and rules used within those forms.

Getting to Know Families and Communities

The value of conversations extends beyond the classroom. It's important to have conversations about the interests of your students with their parents or guardians. And it's important to know your student's community. The work of Luis Moll et al (1992) was a groundbreaking piece of research that highlighted the concept of a student's "funds of knowledge." It demonstrated the importance of gathering information about the knowledges that exist in homes and communities. Awareness of these knowledges provides information about who the student is and what the student brings to a learning situation. While it may not be possible for all educators to replicate learning about students' communities to the depth to which Moll did, it is possible for the teacher to move beyond the walls of the school and to interact with and honor a community by shopping at the local stores, going to see a sporting event, dropping in on a public event or celebration, or attending a funeral.

Some schools are finding success by moving parent–educator meetings out of the school and into community halls, legions, church basements, or other community meeting areas. This practice sends the message that not only does the school value the community that provides support, it also wants to know more about that community.

The key to this participation in your students' community is simply open-minded participation; it's not about judging the community's strengths and weaknesses. Through participation, we engage the community, value the various ways in which knowledge is displayed, and perhaps change our perception of who each student is.

Many schools have a meet-the-teacher event, where the teacher reviews the year's topics of study, and schools that use this time to develop relationships with parents are more likely to begin relationship-building with the community. In short, the meet-the-teacher event should become a meet-the-school community event. To ensure the important messages of school expectations are conveyed, the principal can provide a welcoming introduction and overview; the outlines of specific courses can be provided as handouts and electronically. The rest of the time should focus on conversations among the parents and the educator.

Some parents may not be comfortable with this form of conversation, so provide some other entry points. A electronic or photographic series of images that is posted at a local grocery store or community centre and displays activities, places of interest, or events in the community or school can provide an entry point into a real conversation between parents and teachers. When parents suggest additional areas of interest in the community, consider their input an indication that a connection has been made.

As with any school event, some parents participate and some don't. Don't make assumptions about participation or lack of participation. It's unfair to assume that lack of participation is a reflection of lack of parental interest; it may simply be an indication that a meet-the-teacher gathering might not be the best way to communicate with a particular student's family. It's up to you and the school to work out ways to effectively communicate with parents and guardians.

In one school I know, the principal heard a lot of conversations among parents about Bingo. He realized that attending Bingo games was an important part of the community's social life; he decided to build on this interest by inviting parents to participate in school-sponsored Bingo games. His decision was a good one. The school Bingo game was enjoyed by students, families, and members of the community. The social atmosphere provided opportunities for teachers, parents, and community members to chat and get to know each other as people. Just as building on a student's interests can lead to re-engagement, increased communication between home and school begins with knowing the community's interests and building on them.

Engaging Individual Students in Conversation

Conversations provide powerful information for a educator. A good conversation on a topic of interest can lead to the first insights about a student's interests and funds of knowledge. Keep this information by recording it in your assessment notes; you'll find it a useful reminder of what the student brings to the classroom.

Follow up classroom conversations and conversations with families with individual conversations. If you learn that a student is interested in some form of the visual arts, make a point to ask the student questions about the techniques of his or her favorite medium as you walk in the hall, monitor the cafeteria, or walk with the child to the bus. Your interest in extending the conversation sends a message to the child that you listened to what he or she said, that you were interested enough to take note of the information, and that you want to know more. The key is to make the conversation casual and not a series of questions—that's not a conversation; it's an interrogation.

Here's a hint: be yourself. Don't try to make a connection with students by trying to become the "cool" educator. The students will see right through your façade. Acknowledge that kids have their own way of defining who's cool, and that it doesn't come from an educator's attempt to be one of the gang; it's based on their respect for the educator.

Alternatives to Conversations

Know-Me Collage

Earlier in this chapter, I mentioned that most students are comfortable having conversations—most, but not all. Some students withdraw from conversations and are not comfortable sharing information in that sort of situation. To gather information about these students, an alternative format can be provided. A collage is a good example.

A collage is an assortment of artifacts that provides a visual, auditory, or tactile message about a specific topic. A Know-Me Collage is a way for students to create a collage about themselves. Each student has the freedom to decide on a style of presentation, such as a musical compilation, a collection of electronic or paper images, or a presentation of a variety of surfaces/textures that have meaning to the student.

The sample on page 54, prepared by a teacher as an example to begin the Know-Me Collage lesson, illustrates that point. This Know-Me Collage has the potential to tell you more about that person than many conversations, or even a written biography. Providing students with an opportunity to create a Know-Me Collage allows them to reflect on what they know, their interests, and how best to relay that information. The decision about "how best to relay that information" opens the door to forms of communication other than reading and writing. For some students, that's reason enough to engage.

Remember, getting-to-know-you conversations and exercises aren't just a beginning-of-the-year activity, so keep time open each day for a conversation and take every opportunity to get to know your students. Time can be found first thing in the morning, during transitions between subjects, before recess, or as a way to end the day. You'll be gathering information to inform your planning and building a relationship of respect with your students.

How Well Are You Listening?

Answer each question with *Most of the Time, Sometimes,* or *Not Very Often.* You can draw a picture or write a note below each question.

- Can you make a picture in your mind about what the person is saying?

- Do you want to listen to this person?

- Can you stay calm when you're listening even if the person is angry?

- Do you keep your mind on what the person is saying?

- Do you wait until the person is finished speaking?

- Do you give a solution that makes the person know you listened?

- Do you look at the person and let the person know you are listening?

- Do you ask questions if you don't understand?

Pembroke Publishers © 2010 *Engaging the DisEngaged* by Beth Critchley Charlton ISBN 978-1-55138-258-6

5 Using What You *Know* About Re-engaging Students

Remember the discussion of suggested solutions to disengagement in the Introduction and headlines that call for a complete overhaul of the public school model?

As much as I enjoy conversations about educational change and embrace the opportunities to discuss possibilities, I'm also proud enough of what we do as teachers to state that I don't think a complete overhaul of the public school model is necessary. Still, I'm enough of a realist to accept that change can be forward-moving, and should be an integral part of our practice. But effective change takes time, and it wouldn't be wise to expect the realization of any wide-sweeping goals before the end of this school year. And, every year, it's this year's students who are of primary importance.

But that doesn't mean we have to accept the status quo. By reflecting on and rethinking existing practice within our present educational structures, we inform the ongoing and more realistic goals of educational change.

What We Know About Good Teaching

We begin this process the same way we begin the process of establishing what our students have accomplished. We ask ourselves, "What do we know about good teaching?" The answer to this question leads to what we know about re-engaging the disengaged student.

We know there are common elements among our most successful lessons. Each of us has an established bank of lesson ideas that we know have worked. I often refer to these lessons as "keepers." There are some tried and true lessons that can be adapted for any content and any grade level. When we deconstruct these lessons, we find they have common elements:

- a clear purpose
- a clear and concise presentation
- a focus on thinking, on using information, and on problem-solving
- a high level of expectation
- relevance to the student as a person and as a learner
- the right level of challenge and support
- access to ongoing and honest feedback
- a clear application to other learning situations
- opportunities for varied ways and locations to demonstrate learning
- opportunities for students to demonstrate independence

Looking at Learning

We also know what makes these lessons lead to learning. In simplified form, it's something like this:

1. In an effort to make meaning, we filter information through what we already know. When things make sense, you experience a sense of equilibrium.
2. When you notice that something doesn't make sense, this equilibrium is challenged and questions arise. It's clear that more information is needed.
3. To re-establish equilibrium, you draw on a variety of searching techniques to find the information that allows you to understand or learn from the challenge to your equilibrium. You review what you know, rethink what you know, and search for new information to answer your questions. Searching techniques include accessing and using background knowledge to confirm, challenge, and possibly rethink what we know; asking questions of people who have more information than we do; and using other sources, such as books, or visual or digital media, to access additional information.
4. Once the equilibrium seems to be re-established, you check to ensure that the new information is meaningful and applicable.
5. You use that information in a variety of ways and it becomes a part of what you know.

Here's an example: Throughout this book, you've been able to read and understand the text. Through reading and understanding, you've experienced equilibrium and disequilibrium as you agreed with, questioned, applied, or disagreed with various sections or statements. And now you see this:

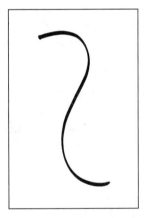

The placement of this squiggle on this page causes a disequilibrium. It appears to be a meaningless squiggle on the page. But if I tell you that this squiggle is the only remaining part of an old, faded illustration, you have a context in which to place the squiggle. You start to search for possibilities of what the original illustration could have been:

- Is it a part of a letter in a word?
- Is it a part of a map?
- Is it part of a portrait?

After suggesting a few possibilities, you realize that you don't have enough information, that your search for answers is simply guessing and there's no way to check for correctness. You need more information. In this case, your only source for that information is the next clue, which is this: The illustration was originally a Barnum and Bailey poster.

If you have background knowledge about Barnum and Bailey, you know that the poster is connected to a circus theme. You run some options through your mind. You check by looking back at the squiggle and realize that a meaningful possibility is an elephant's trunk. At that point, the meaning of this squiggle becomes very clear (and the really interesting thing is that, all of a sudden, you can also even see, hear, and smell the elephant and the circus surroundings.) If you don't have background knowledge about Barnum and Bailey, your search needs to widen. You require more information to ensure that you have a response that makes sense. And then, as an expert learner, you would still insist on checking your information with a source that confirms it or someone who knows the correct answer. I'm that person, and I'm telling you that you are correct.

In simplest possible terms, that's the thinking process that leads to learning. It's active and engaging. The next task is to find ways to engage all students in thinking as an active process.

Putting It Together

Reflecting on what we know about teaching and learning allows us to face the onslaught of information and suggestions about how to improve our practice. Each day, I receive at least 20 articles, advertisements, or free trial offers that claim to be the miracles I need to close the achievement gap, solve the gender issue, or re-establish classroom control. They don't ever live up to their claims and I think that's because they focus on some components of good teaching and effective learning, but fail to consolidate all we know about teaching and learning. And, as explored in Chapter 2, their claims often present a deficit view of fixing what's wrong instead of building on what's working.

The characteristic learning pattern of disengaged students is to accumulate bits and pieces of information as they fade in and out of engagement. It's up to us to figure out how to fit those bits and pieces fit together. A positive perspective coupled with an educator's expertise in the developmental steps of learning and the curriculum expectations will provide the insight needed to begin planning. The first step of planning is to link the student's interests and funds of knowledge with the information we have about the student's knowledge of "school stuff."

With "What does this student have under control?" as the first question, we have a starting point; remember, the perspective through which we view student work is the perspective of what the student knows. So, if a 12-year-old student reads at a lower text level than the expectations for his or her age, our concern is not how far behind the student is or what this student's weaknesses in reading are. Our only concern is that we have the instructional tools and knowledge to meet this student where he or she is and provide solid instruction that moves the student forward. If, despite our best efforts, we are not leading this student to ongoing progress, it's our responsibility to search out different instructional methods that will better match who the student is as a learner.

Once that's accepted, we have the freedom to explore possibilities and find an instructional model that matches the student, content that engages the student, and continuous observation to ensure that the student moves forward.

These sample questions illustrate how to link the teacher's knowledge about the student as a person to the subject knowledge of the curriculum. The student in this example is in junior high. As the teacher chatted with and observed the student, she used sticky notes (see page 36) to make a record of the student's interests. Through her note-taking, the teacher knew this student had a strong interest in a wide range of sports. The teacher used the sticky notes to match the student's interests with subject area content. Here's an example of her thinking:

- Question: What are the mathematics, suited to this child's knowledge of mathematics, of this sport?
  Junior High Curriculum Links: performance statistics, probability, complex computations
- Question: What is the history, suited to this child's knowledge of history, of this sport?
  Junior High Curriculum Links: sport in early civilizations, a sport's development through history
- Question: What are the associations, suited to this child's knowledge of the arts, between the arts and this sport?
  Junior High Curriculum Links: art in early civilizations, portraying movement through the arts
- Question: What media, social, or written text is associated with this sport?
  Junior High Curriculum Links: a critical analysis of the coverage of doping scandals

As lessons in specific topics were planned, the teacher began with these real-life applications of information and infused these applications into the lesson.

These infusions provide a reason for an initial engagement and continued engagement throughout a unit of study, and can have significant impact on sustaining engagement. Mihaly Csikszentmihalyi (Scherer, 2002) provides an example how a formerly disengaged student's newfound interest in Japanese fishponds led him, at the age of 18, to start a koi pond business:

…he felt tremendous. He had to learn everything from plumbing to biology: how the fish live and what to feed them. He learned chemistry. He learned mathematics to understand water pressure and volume. Senior year he did great in school. He ended up going to a community college and taking technical courses.

Csikszentmihalyi goes on to describe his personal view of what education should be: education should provide students with opportunities to explore a wide range of interests until they make "a connection between something inside and something outside." It's that connection we use to move the student forward.

Instruction that Moves the Student Forward

See Looking at Learning on page 58.

Once a student's areas of interest are known, instruction that moves the student forward is instruction that leads to effective independent learning strategies. Effective learning strategies provide the student with the knowledge to notice when things don't make sense, to search for new information in a variety of ways, and to check that the information used re-establishes meaning. It's about learning how to think and then learning how to use thinking effectively.

This process was described by Costa and Kallick (2000) as the Habits of Mind. The habits of mind present thinking as an intellectual behavior. The word *behavior* suggests an active rather than a passive response to information. Becoming aware of the different ways to approach information allows students to see

Costa and Kallick (2000) identify 16 Habits of Mind:

- persisting
- thinking and communicating with clarity and precision
- managing impulsivity
- gathering data through all the senses
- listening with understanding and empathy
- creating, imaging, and innovating
- thinking flexibly
- responding with wonderment and awe
- thinking about thinking
- taking responsible risks
- striving for accuracy
- finding humor
- questioning and posing problems
- thinking interdependently
- applying past knowledge to new situations
- remaining open to continuous learning

As you go thorough the ideas on thinking with different subjects, make note of the connections between the content of the lesson and the Habits of Mind.

beyond the notion of "lesson as content to be remembered" to an understanding of "lesson as information to be used."

Developing Lessons with a Focus on Thinking

The ideas presented here focus on thinking. They build on the idea of understanding what the student brings to the learning situation and using that information in a wide variety of ways.

To prepare for lessons with a focus on thinking, read the eight words presented below.

Know teaching, Know progress
No teaching, No progress

Have a discussion with your colleagues about the meaning of these words and the process you used to arrive at that meaning. Compare the content of your conversation with Costa and Kallick's Habits of Mind to get a sense of your intellectual behavior.

Keep a record of your conversation and use it with the words below to demonstrate the process of thinking to your students.

Know sports, Know health
No sports, No health

Remind your students that thinking is an active process that unfolds, not an impulse reaction that remains static.

It's a simple activity, but it provides students with an awareness of thinking as a process. Build other Know/No patterns with your students. Here are a few ideas that have been suggested by my students:

Know Facebook, Know Friends
No Facebook, No Friends? (note that the insertion of the question mark opens this up to debate)

Know fashion, Know style
No fashion, No style

Know conflict, Know anger
No conflict, No anger

Thinking with the Arts

The arts, expressed through movement, images, sounds, tactile experiences, and tastes, infiltrate much of a student's life. Think of the visual, dramatic, and movement arts that often fill a student's out-of-school time—music, dance, fashion, drawing, or building Lego creations. They all provide definition to a student's out-of-school of life. It's such a foundational piece of their being that we should take advantage of that foundation and build on it.

Don't, as was traditional practice, leave the arts to the end of a unit of study. While it's true that the students who have disengaged may re-engage for this new experience, it is a fleeting engagement and the unit of study has already passed them by.

Students who appear to be disengaged from reading may simply be disengaged from *school* reading. This photograph can easily lead to an out-of-school exploration of text—its wide range of forms, formats, and purposes.

We know the arts engage students, so access to the arts in our schools should be a priority. To begin, review your subject area content and process strands with an eye for opportunities to include thinking through the arts. You'll find a wide range of math, history, and language arts lessons can be developed from a work of art, a piece of music, or the movements of dance.

Student's Area of Interest: Visual Arts: Photography

Look at the photograph and use the procedure shown on page 60.

- Question: What is the mathematics, suited to this child's knowledge of photography, of this photograph?
  Elementary Curriculum Links: geometry (study of angles, nonstandard units to calculate area)
- Question: What is a social studies topic, suited to this child's knowledge of photography, of this photograph?
  Elementary Curriculum Links: representations of popular culture
- Question: What is a science topic, suited to this child's knowledge of photography, of this photograph?
  Secondary School Curriculum Links: study of light (shadows and time); depth of field

- Question: What are media, social, or written texts, suited to this child's knowledge of photography, of this photograph?
  Secondary School Curriculum Links: critical literacy; various representations of information; defining acceptable and unacceptable messages

Student's Area of Interest: Music

To rethink mathematics instruction for a student interested in music, connect knowledge of the student's favorite genre to various content areas. For example, if that choice is rock music, we know that the student is thinking about rock music, so teach lessons that apply that thinking.

- Question: What is the mathematics, suited to this child's knowledge of music, of the musical genre of rock music?
  Middle School Curriculum Links: timing and pattern (the mathematics of the rhythm of the music); estimation and calculation (the mathematics of the business of a concert)
- Question: What is a social studies topic, suited to this child's knowledge of music, of the musical genre of rock music?
  Middle School Curriculum Links: cultural studies (the roots and development of rock music)
- Question: What is a science topic, suited to this child's knowledge of music, suited to this child's knowledge of music, of the musical genre of rock music?
  Middle School Curriculum Links: sound; the physics of pyrotechnics
- Question: What are media, social, or written texts, suited to this child's knowledge of music, suited to this child's knowledge of music, of the musical genre of rock music?
  Middle School Curriculum Links: critical literacy (analyzing lyrics); comparative literature (the study of songs and song writers)

Once you begin, the list of possibilities goes on and on. The expertise of the teacher is needed to ensure that lessons provide the student the opportunity to build on his or her knowledge in ways that extend thinking and provide connections to the next steps of learning.

Thinking with Movement

We know that some disengaged students are pent-up bundles of energy, searching for ways to express that energy. The classroom routine of sitting for long periods of time is often the source of their disengagement. Opportunities to move "inside, outside, upside down" (thanks to Dr. Seuss) provide chances to use that pent-up energy in ways that renew involvement in thinking and learning. Building on the theme of using the arts, the use of dance and all forms of movement provides many students who are present in the classroom but are disengaged from the lesson with a reason to re-engage. Physical activity in any form, within and outside the boundaries of the classroom and school walls, provides automatic connections to many of a student's interests.

For example, how often does a student say his or her favorite subject is physical education? If we think that this is simply because physical education provides a reason to play, we're seriously misjudging the learning that occurs in the gym and on the sports field. The purpose of physical education is exactly the same as the purpose of any subject, which is to develop the ability to access and use knowledge to think and problem-solve. In physical education, those lessons are taught through movement. The fact that it is so popular simply demonstrates that movement has the power to engage. With some planning, any subject can be explored by leaving the desk.

If you are concerned that increased movement might lead to chaos, rethink that concern through a perspective of what works. Make note of which movement activities most engage the students and search for ways to connect them to lessons. Involving the students in the planning process gives them a vested interest in creating a successful and nonchaotic lesson. Once students become used to possibilities for movement and feel the success associated with learning something new, they will begin to see movement as a part of the class routine and not as "special" time that provides an opportunity to misbehave.

The movement associated with dance or sport opens the door to lessons in all subject areas. For example, matching dance or a sport with social studies leads to

- the origins of the dance/sport
- comparing the historical nature of the dance/sport to present versions
- the meaning of the costumes/uniforms associated with the dance/sport
- the cultural relevance of the dance/sport
- the location and geography of the country of origin of the dance/sport
- the social and political history of the country of origin of the dance/sport

A wonderful example of a teacher's use of movement occurred when I was in Grade 6. During that year, we all made marble mazes at home—by hammering nails into a maze pattern on a 16" x 16" piece of plywood—and brought them to school. During our recess break, we each would challenge a friend to weave a marble through our mazes. Depending on where the marble landed, the player won or lost a certain number of marbles. (Looking back, I realize it was an early—almost Stone Age—version of PacMan.) As time went on, my classmates brought in mazes of ever-increasing difficulty.

Our teacher watched our games and made use of our interest in and ability to plan and create mazes. She arrived one day with a full sheet of plywood and hundreds of nails of all sizes. She told us it was time to put our maze-making skills to a new use. We were to create a relief map of Canada. Our first step was to research the elevations of the various zones of Canadian geography and then calculate which nail size would represent each elevation. Once the calculations were completed, we hammered in the nails, which provided the underpinnings for the next project: using papier mâché to cover the entire surface of the map. It was a year-long project. Our teacher provided the necessary start points and questions for each lesson and we did all of the research and building. This was an entirely new learning experience for us (after all, it was 1967) and we loved every minute of it. We were researching, planning, problem-solving, and building. Each element of the project required movement. I clearly remember that two students who had been formerly disengaged from most class work decided to lead the activity. They led us well. Throughout the year, we learned lessons about geography, math, and reading that stay with me still. This lesson also stands out as the type that has held up throughout the years. Today, this kind of lesson is much more common, but no less effective. If we compare this lesson to the list of what we know about good lessons (page 57), we can see why.

Thinking with Technology

The world of technology provides us with every possible opportunity to think. All we need to do is make sure that we're using technology to encourage the full process of thinking, and not simply for endless searching.

The TED (Technology, Entertainment and Design) conferences began in 1984, springing up from a desire to provide a venue for "ideas worth spreading." The TED website provides students with access to the thinkers of our times. The Creators project is another site that offers students contact with people who are exploring ideas. A visit to TED, the Creators Project, or the many and varied student podcast sites allows students to listen and observe the thinking of others and to value how different our interests and thought processes are.

Engagement often begins with an opportunity to listen and observe. When including visits to "thinking sites" in your lessons, allow time for students to do just that—listen and observe. Exposure to a variety of ideas and ways to express those ideas opens new doors and creates options for all learners, particularly those who are disengaged.

The Thinking Fair

Remember that learning also occurs beyond the school walls. Take advantage of the community to visit people and places of interest.

With each opportunity for students to listen and observe, make note of the types of topics that hold the interest of the students. Those are the topics that go into the building of the Thinking Fair. A Thinking Fair builds on the established and very successful Science Fairs that are held regularly in schools. In a Thinking Fair, students are encouraged to find a topic of interest and use a variety of research sources (community members, library, Internet, and subject-area knowledge) to develop their thoughts around that topic. The presentation format can be electronic or live, and can include whatever visual, auditory, written, or movement-based presentation style appeals to the student. The Thinking Fair develops thinking and provides learning that intersects with all subject areas. It also provides an opportunity for students, educators, parents, and community members to share their thinking, which opens and widens the thinking of other students, educators, and community members.

Thinking with Debates

A debate on a subject of interest is perhaps one of the most authentic activities in which a student can participate. Although perceived by the novice observer as an argument (let's face it, that's part of the appeal), a debate is actually a wonderful opportunity to encourage students to refine their thinking and problem-solving strategies. To debate successfully, one must thoroughly understand the topic, establish a position, and defend that position in a manner that convinces others to respect and possibly share one's opinion. Here's what students need to know about debates.

What Is a Debate?

A debate is a formal argument about a stated resolution. There are always two sides:
- The pro side—this side collects information to affirm the resolution.
- The con side—this side collects information to argue against the resolution.

What Is the Goal of a Debate?

The goal of a debate is to win the argument, not to reach a compromise.

How Do I Prepare for a Debate?

The graphic organizer on page 81 can be used to demonstrate how prepare for a debate.

- Find all the information you can about both sides of the resolution.
- Decide which information is the strongest information and why.
- Try to think about how the other team will approach the debate.
- Practice your listening skills and your oral presentation skills.
- Always think about what you know and how it can be used in the debate.

What Happens During a Debate?

In a debate, there are rules about who speaks and when they speak. Here is one simple debate pattern that can be used at all grade levels:

1. Opening
   - A person on the pro team gives the reason for agreeing with the resolution.
   - A person on the con team gives the reason for being against the resolution.
2. Argument (Rebuttal)
   - A person on the pro team argues against specific points raised by the con team.
   - A person on the con team argues against specific points raised by the pro team.
3. Conclusion
   - A person on the pro team summarizes their main arguments and the flaws in the con team's argument.
   - A person on the con team summarizes their main arguments and the flaws in the pro team's argument.
4. Judgment
   - An impartial judge declares a winner.

Thinking through Connecting

Learning occurs when we are able to connect new knowledge with what is already known in a way that makes sense. Without this connection, a student learns only pieces of information, the use or purpose of which may not be clear. Information without a purpose does little to engage a student.

Connection Collection

To connect the new to the known, we use our background knowledge and our experiences to position and consider new information. We ask if the new information connects, how it connects, where it connects, and why it connects. A Connection Collection provides students with an opportunity to see how new information connects to what they know and allows them to develop their thinking about that topic.

A Connection Collection is presented as a grid (see sample on page 67) filled with a variety of nouns, verbs, adjectives, and adverbs. The task is to think about how the words can be connected and then organized into a story, song, or poem.

To begin, cover each word on the Connection Collection with a sticky note and place the Connection Collection on the overhead projector. Uncover one word and demonstrate, through a think-aloud, your connection to that word. Uncover another word and make a connection between it and the previous word.

There's no need to uncover words sequentially; any order is fine. As you continue to lift each sticky note, build your connections into some sort of text form. Let the students know that, at this point, you're simply getting a rough idea of what your story is going to be about.

Once you've demonstrated the process, show the class a new Connection Collection (for younger students, four to six cells are enough). Tell them that it's now their job to make the connections and organize the connections into a story. As you lift the sticky notes off each word, the students *silently* make connections to create their own stories. Once all the cells are exposed, give the students a minute or so to put their thoughts together and then ask them to share their stories. As each student shares his or her story, poem, or song, use an overhead marker to trace the path the student is using to connect the words. Use a different-colored marker to trace the order in which each student connects the words. After four or five sharings, the class sees a wonderful array of possibilities for connecting words into ideas. It's a terrific visual representation of thinking and a demonstration of the different ways we each use the same information.

Here are two examples using the same Connection Collection:

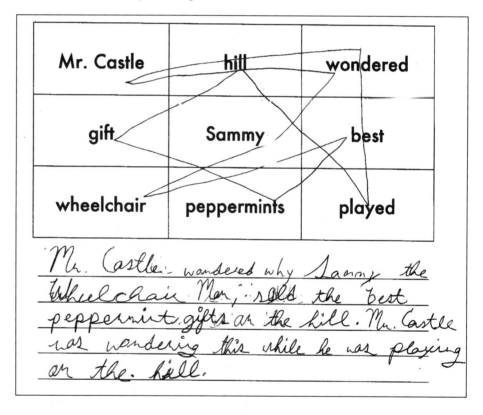

It's interesting to note that this student chose to track the direction of his thinking by connecting the words right on the grid.

By Zoe

While climbing up the hill, I ~~found~~ Date

I wondered why peppermints were
such a strange gift. it is still
the best gift. I found out I needed
a wheelchair for Sammy AKA
Mr. Castle. After, I played with
Mr. Wheelchair.

—Mr Castle wondered why Sammy had the
best wheelchair with peppermints as
wheels. Sammy got the gift when he
played soccer on the hill

Both students produced these pieces of writing within minutes. Both were keen to discuss how to add more detail and to reorganize their thoughts. After discussion, the student who wrote the second sample decided to begin the second story with an image that came to her during our discussion. This is clear evidence of how the Connection Collection can be one way to engage student writers. Once a student is engaged in the task, we have the information we need to sustain that engagement.

The next sample is an example of a nonfiction Connection Collection. The topic was brought to my attention by my colleague Karla Walker. While discussing a student's interest in eye make-up, we built connections between this interest, a history lesson on ancient Egypt, and a mathematics lesson in geometry. Together, Karla and I created this Connection Collection. The student's task was to use these words as the source of her research about the history of make-up.

Connection Collection: The Shape of Cleopatra's Make-up

protection	green	kohl pots	fade
scalene	Cleopatra	malachite	arch
henna	brow	black	angles

The student first worked with the words that had meaning to her (black, brow, henna, arch, green) and then searched a variety of sources to place the remaining words in the context of Cleopatra's make-up. While increasing her knowledge about make-up, the student was surprised to learn about the precision with which make-up is applied: that the scalene triangle is the foundation of the line that creates the cat's-eye shape for eyeliner, and that the arch of an eyebrow was a mathematical calculation. Through the Connection Collection, this student's geometry lessons now had a purpose.

The simplicity of the Connection Collection is what makes it so effective. In addition to using it as a base for a lesson, it can be used as an assessment tool; it's a wonderful way to gain insight into how a student connects the important items of information presented, and provides the teacher with information about what's known and where to go next.

Keep some blank Connection Collections in a writing or speaking centre. Students might want to create their own word grids and pair up with a classmate. Using the same words, each student creates his or her own story. Then they can compare stories and explain how their connections were made. As levels of complexity increase, words can be replaced with phrases, dialogue, etc.

Time for you to try one. Take a minute to use the Connection Collection below to connect the words associated with the title of this book, *Engaging the Disengaged*. Remember to think and connect through the perspective of the potential that is reflected in the book's key question, *What Do You Know?* Connect the words in any order that works for you.

See page 82 for a Connection Collection template.

conversation	gender	risk	family
observing	thinking	foundation	student
engagement	community	assessment	knowledge

Share your connections with a colleague; it will open the door to conversations about how to engage students.

Re-engaging Students with Reading

Up to this point, little has been said about reading and writing instruction, but that's not meant to minimize its importance. Until students see the purpose for reading and writing, *and* can handle the demands of the text associated with any lesson, they will not be fully engaged. So solid instruction in reading and writing, and not simply helping students to read, is not only essential to a disengaged student, it is also the right of every student.

Reading is an active process of making sense of text. Reading is not simply knowing how to decode words efficiently, and it's not simply understanding the literal messages of text. I can decode words in French very well and I can also make some sense of text written in French, but I can't read French. To read, one must have a facility with a variety of problem-solving strategies that go beyond word-solving to understanding and meaning-making with range and depth.

When students have difficulty reading the text provided in a lesson, it's our responsibility to make text more accessible. This is accomplished through instruction, not through compensatory procedures such as text on tape or a more-skilled partner reading to a less-skilled partner. These adaptations might be useful for completing the day's assignment, but they are short-term measures; it's crucial that educators search for new ways to allow students to re-engage in reading instruction and to maintain that engagement.

Re-engagement comes from rethinking reading instruction. Although educators revel in or rail against specific instructional techniques and can quote from years of research conducted by the most respected researchers, the truth is that no one instructional technique works for all students. What does make a difference is the educator's awareness of what the student has under control, the many and varied instructional techniques and the educator's flexibility in the use of every piece of knowledge at his or her disposal.

There are many ways a student's reading development can unfold:

- Some students simply require access to text and the process of reading seems to magically develop. Given just a few hints and well-timed lessons along the way, these readers fully engage in the "whole" of reading and take delight in discovering the layers of meaning and the application of the information in what they read.
- Some students require explicit instruction in how to process meaning and then how to work toward word-solving. These readers seem to use their background knowledge, picture clues, and knowledge of story structure to make sense of text. As demands for word-solving increase, these students need instruction in the *how-to*s of root words, affixes, and syllables.
- Some students require explicit, almost mathematically precise, instruction in word-solving, and then build up to processing meaning from text. These are the students who appear to thrive with specific instruction in phonics. These students go from part to whole, and with good instruction are able to consolidate the units of sound into words, phrases, and sentences that work together meaningfully.
- Some students require explicit instruction that uses bits and pieces of all of the above.

That's why deciding how to teach a student to read is perhaps one of the most challenging and the most exciting components of teaching.

But the first step in effective reading instruction is the same for all students. The first step is a reading assessment, designed, administered, and scored from the perspective of determining what the student can do. The reading record described in Chapter 3 is one way to gather this information. A discussion with the student about how he or she approaches text is the next step. From there, the teacher plans lessons that build on the student's use of text clues and problem-solving strategies.

Regardless of the instructional process used, I'm fairly comfortable saying that the more a student reads (really *reads*, not just decodes), the more he or she knows. To re-engage a student in reading, the content of the text must engage the student as a person and as a pupil, and the reading level of the text needs to be accessible to that student. In most classes, that means we need a wide range of reading material at a wide range of levels of text difficulty.

For text to be accessible, a student should be able to handle 90+% of the words on the page, process the information at a flexible, fluent rate, and demonstrate understanding. This high degree of accuracy may seem a tall order but, in my experience, it's the key to re-engaging a reader. At 90% accuracy, the student can focus thinking on the meaning of the text. Having a solid grasp on the meaning allows the student to enter into the solving of difficult words with knowledge of the context and structure of the passage. The context and structure of the passage make the syllable, affix, and letter work much more effective. Perhaps even more important for a disengaged reader is that, at 90+% accuracy, the student "hears success" and knows that he or she *can* read.

The Nonfiction Vertical File

Even more important than providing a student with accessible text is providing text that the student is interested in. Here's an idea for providing students with a wide range of engaging and topical text topics at a wide range of difficulty levels.

I spent my university years working in the library at the Maritime School of Social Work. One of my responsibilities was to keep the library's vertical file up to date. The vertical file was a cabinet full of current newspaper and magazine clippings on topics of interest to the students and faculty of the school. Each day, I reviewed the local, national, and international press for articles of interest. As part-time jobs go, it was a pretty good one. (Looking back, I guess I was amassing the information of a "Google Alert" when the whole idea of Google wasn't even a sparkle in some computer programmer's eye.)

Years later, I used the idea of the vertical file for my students. I found a plastic file box, file folders, and dividers. I asked the students about their interests and, for the next few weeks, I scoured libraries for every magazine and newspaper available in a search for articles on topics of interest.

In addition to collecting a wide range of articles on each topic, I also searched for a wide range of levels of reading difficulty. It was my goal to provide a successful reading experience for every student. Success was defined as the ability to comfortably read a variety of texts written about a variety of topics of interest. For example, there were times when an article had a font or illustrations that appeared too childish for the intended reader. In these cases, I retyped the article in the standard font of text books.

The vertical file was well-received by the students. As they looked through the articles, they realized that I had listened carefully to their requests for reading material. Evidence that a teacher listens carries a lot of weight with students. Some days, the vertical file was for browsing; other times, I used the text as the foundation for a lesson about a reading strategy. After the lesson, students were expected to choose an article of interest from the vertical file, apply the lesson, and formulate a response. Responses varied from written to oral to visual.

Remember that reading lessons are important. We would be naïve to think that, simply by providing articles of interest at a specific text level, a child's reading will improve. Students who have disengaged from reading need to make up a fair amount of ground, and solid reading instruction is the only way for that to happen.

It was at this point that the project became most satisfying, because the students who were formerly disengaged from reading became engaged. Some of the most memorable moments of my teaching career have come from classes where the vertical file was in use. One student who had formerly avoided reading called out, "I claim the article about the boxer." Another student with a solid distaste for reading refused to choose an article, so an article—on a topic I assumed to be of interest and at a comfortable reading level—was provided to him. I watched as he slid low in his desk, the article on his lap. But as he started to read, his posture changed; he straightened up and placed the article on his desk. He looked up at me and tried his hardest not to smile. Upon finishing, he said, "Ya got anymore of these? I know it's easy, but I can understand it." Now that's an open door to re-engagement!

"I know it's easy, but I can understand it." Talk about self-assessment! I chatted with the student about what he meant when he said the article was easy. He said, "It's not as hard as the stuff the other kids are reading, but it's the first time I've

I realize now that a collaborative effort that included other teachers, students, and members of the school community would have greatly facilitated this process. I also would suggest a web-based vertical file, with active links to sites of interest.

Browsing time, when students have the opportunity to engage with text of interest at any level of difficulty, is an important complement to instructional reading time.

read anything in years." I knew that we had found this student's solid foundation in reading and that it was my job to provide the lesson—and just the right amount of pressure and support—to scaffold on this foundation. Forward ho!

Re-engaging Students with Writing

For all the same reasons you provide solid reading instruction, you should provide solid writing instruction as an important part of a child's day in school. Students have a right to learn how to write. Like re-engagement in reading, re-engagement in writing instruction begins with the educator's knowledge of the student as a person.

Once we know our students, their interests, and their funds of knowledge, we have the topics for our writing lessons and a variety of purposes for them as well. Think of writing instruction as a way to teach students to communicate with and about what is important to them. Regardless of the age of your student, choose a genre that matches the student. For example, being able to write persuasively is just as useful to a seven-year-old who wishes to voice an opinion about the rules of the playground as it is to the 16-year-old who disagrees with the new cafeteria policies about healthy foods. Both have a use for a lesson on persuasive writing, only the depth of technique and level of argument expected need to be adjusted.

The Interest Bank

To determine topics and genres that match a student's interests, begin with the development of a personal Interest Bank. An Interest Bank is a series of guiding questions that encourage a student to think about, talk about, and write about areas of potential interest. It's successful, because the ideas start from real experience.

Bringing the Ideas Forward

The lesson begins with an interview between you and a willing student or visiting adult. The questions should be adjusted to reflect the age of the student. The interview questions reflect an area of the interviewee's interest; in this case, an interest in hockey.

1. *You've told me that you have an interest in hockey. When did that interest begin?*
2. *Can you describe something about hockey that you just can't forget?*
3. *What's something about hockey that you really like?*
4. *What's something about hockey you really don't like?*
5. *Who is a hockey player that you respect? Why?*
6. *What is something that you'd like to change about hockey (in the world, in your life, in school)?*
7. *Is there a recent controversy in hockey? Tell us about it.*

As you conduct the interview, the role of the students in the class is to listen; the interview is not time for other students to comment on the answers. The message is that, through listening, we absorb information that enriches our own ideas. After the interview, thank the class for listening so well.

To re-engage the disengaged writer, leave story writing to those who have an interest. No matter how exciting the story starter might seem you, it's simply not of interest to some students. The need or desire to write a story might develop over time.

The Interest Bank in this lesson is based on Nanci Atwell's work.

Before beginning this interview, make sure that you know your class well. If, in your awareness of their backgrounds, there is a question that might cause a student to feel uncomfortable, omit it or change it.

Getting the Ideas Flowing

The graphic organizer provided on page 83 allows for insertion of student-specific topics. This planning takes extra time, but demonstrating to the child that you are acknowledging who he or she is as a person is time well-spent. As an alternative, you can hand out the incomplete form and encourage students to fill in the blanks with their own interest(s).

Discuss the format with the students—the questions are presented in a grid because full sentences are unnecessary; this grid is just for jot-notes about ideas. Questions can be answered in any order. Make it clear to students that they won't have to share this idea bank with their classmates; it is for each student's personal use only. This chart is for recording personal thoughts, feelings, and experiences that might eventually become fodder for writing.

As students work on their Interest Banks, circulate and chat with them. Some students might need to have the meaning of questions clarified. If students are stuck, don't feel you have to give them ideas; it's more effective to guide their thinking by asking questions that provide support. Not all students will answer all questions—that's okay. This is just a start point. Once the students have worked for a while, have them close the folders. You decide how much work is enough for that day. Closing the folders doesn't stop the thinking, but means that the thoughts will continue in their heads.

Choosing an Idea and Writing

Don't worry if a student chooses the same genre many times; that student is re-establishing his or her level of comfort with writing and might need the comfort of this genre to continue. Over time and with exposure to a wide range of genres (through read-alouds, web searches, drama, etc.) the student will move on.

For the next session, ask the students to look over their notes and choose an idea that "grabs" them as the most interesting. Ask them to do a quick write. Quick writes encourage students to get some ideas on paper, but there's no commitment to develop the ideas, and students have the freedom to choose whatever genre or form of writing they wish. The time for writing is short. After ten minutes, collect the writing folders that contain the Interest Bank and first quick writes. If students resist and want to keep writing, be quietly delighted, but keep the time short. The idea is to leave them wanting more.

Each quick write is dated and kept in the personal writing folder. Through the quick writes, the student is creating a personal idea bank, since every piece of writing is seen as a potential draft for future consideration. The expectation is that, over time and before a clearly articulated date, each student will find an idea among their many drafts that he or she decides is worth developing.

After each opportunity to write, review each student's writing. To provide a forward direction for future lessons, make sure your notes reflect what the student has under control in the elements of the genre and in the traits of writing. Make sure you give each trait its due. As you review each piece of writing, ask yourself the following questions:

- What are the elements that define this genre? To what level are those elements under control?
- What is the student's topic or idea? To what level has the student provided information about that idea and support to that idea?
- How has the student decided to organize his or her writing? To what level has the student demonstrated that organization?
- How has the student chosen the words, phrases, and sentences to express ideas? To what level does word choice create a meaningful impact on the message?

73

- Does the student use an identifiable voice in the writing? To what level has awareness of this voice been developed?
- Does the student's use of conventions, such as spelling, spacing, and punctuation, enhance the clarity of the message? To what level has the student demonstrated his knowledge of conventions?

Following up on the last bullet, don't let the impact of spelling, spacing, and punctuation errors prevent you from acknowledging the message the child has written and level of achievement the student has attained within each trait. There are often wonderful messages behind inaccurate spelling and messy printing.

Provide students with individual feedback about what you notice about their writing and ask them what they've noticed about their writing. This is the information, together with your knowledge of the curriculum and the developmental stages of learning, that is used to plan the next forward step of writing instruction.

After the quick writes are handed in, remind the students that over the next few weeks their writing folders will be filled with lots of ideas on all sorts of topics. Each one represents a possibility. And one of those possibilities will develop into a completed piece of writing on a topic and in a genre that has meaning to the student. A piece of writing that has meaning to the student provides the teacher with information about what the student can do as a writer, and is likely to be the springboard into more engagement in writing.

A Question of Commitment

The process outlined here makes writing instruction seem easy, but it may not be. Not every student will suddenly decide that writing is worth the time and effort. So, what do we do if a student doesn't complete an assignment? (*If*? Perhaps *when* would be a better word, because there will always be incomplete assignments.) The issue of incomplete work needs to be addressed before the lessons begin. Consequences for incomplete work are crucial, so establish them early (with input from the students), then stick to them. Disengaged students, perhaps more than any other students, need to see evidence of work completed and evidence of work well done.

Some educators have concerns about the number of quick writes that are not seen to completion. It might seem that expectations are being lowered rather than raised. This isn't so. The student who has disengaged from writing needs an alternative entrance into the process of writing. The established methods of writing instruction, which are successful with many, just haven't engaged these students. These students need an opportunity to try things without always committing to them. It's been my experience that focused, short, in-class assignments allow students to not only see what they're able to do, they also allow them to see how each piece of writing highlights something they've learned. Yes, the assignment might be shorter than usual, and the result might look like more of a social media text than an essay, but the fact that these students complete an assignment shows a lot more involvement and success than a pattern of missing or incomplete assignments. That's how re-engagement begins.

What Do We Know Now?

This last chapter has provided some ideas and activities to re-spark an interest about and an engagement in school, but building a lesson around an idea or activity provides engagement that is short-lived. To make a difference to a

Starting from what a student has under control is like "divining an underground stream." (Lord, 2007)

student, engagement has to be sustained. To implement these ideas successfully, it's important to keep in mind the messages of knowing the student as a person and a pupil and to provide carefully planned lessons that begin with and then scaffold on what the student knows and is interested in. Your teaching then goes beyond the activity to the application of the information in situations that are meaningful and useful to the student.

Planning Next-Steps Instruction

See page 84 for the Planning Next-Steps Instruction template.

Here is a schematic for planning next-steps lesson for an individual student, for a group of students, or for a whole class.

Date:	
Individual Lesson: *Insert name of student*	Group Lesson: *Insert names of students in group*
Whole-class lesson: *(record absences only)*	

What do I know about the student(s)?
Insert notes about what the student/s has/have under control and how this lesson matches his/her/their interests and background knowledge. This section answers the question, "What does this student know?"

Next-Steps Lesson Focus:
Insert topic of lesson, matched to curriculum expectations. This section answers the question, "Where am I going with this lesson?"

Text/Materials Needed:
Insert all necessary materials in order of use. Ensure there is a match between the student as a person and the student as a learner. This section answers the question, "Do the content and form of the lesson's text and the accompanying materials provide a link between the student and the lesson?"

Procedure:
Insert an overview of the lesson, always thinking about how this lesson is different from previous exposures to the same topic. Make note of how to provide the student with the strategies and skills needed to complete the task independently. Once your notes are written, review them to ensure that the level of educator talk never overtakes the level of student participation. During the lesson, monitor class participation carefully and make contact with individual students. This section answers the question, "How will this lesson engage the students?"

Assessment of Assignment:
Assessment begins at the start of the lesson by providing the student with the expectations of the lesson. Score the assignment from the perspective of what the student knew at the beginning of the lesson and what the student knows at the end of the lesson. This section answers the question, "How will I know what the student learned?"

Notes:
Insert observations and planning notes to inform the next lesson. Making note of the moments of increased engagement provides information about which elements engage which students. Keep these patterns and trends in mind for future planning. This section answers the question, "What did I learn from this lesson about my students and how am I going to use that information?"

Evidence of an engaging lesson: "There was nothing finer than the feeling that came rushing through you when it clicked and you suddenly understood something that had puzzled you." (Walls, 2009)

Learning from Our Own Lessons

Good teaching
- is reflected in successful lessons
- develops student independence
- is not equated with the amount of time the educator spends talking

Each section of the planning template outlined on page 75 reminds the teacher
- to know the student
- to build and not fix
- to move toward independence

The Procedure section of the lesson plan template on page 75 mentions the importance of planning a lesson that is different from those used in the past. But we have to be careful with the word *different*. Something that we've done very well, which is to convey to our students that everyone learns differently, has two meanings for a student, depending on who is being referred to. When a student speaks of another student as learning in a different way, the speaker means it in a positive way. Students today are much better equipped to see their classmates as a wide range of learners. But while they see others in this positive light, they don't always apply the same meaning of *different* to themselves. When a student is aware that he or she learns differently from how classmates do, it is often interpreted as an indication that he or she is *less than* or *not as good as* classmates. It's important that we're prepared for the times when students make comments that indicate that they feel they are not able to keep up with their classmates. This sort of comment usually comes after students have noticed, probably for some time, that their work is not the same as that of their peers.

Throughout this book, we've been trying to define and achieve that change of perspective—that "aha" moment—that improves our teaching practice and helps us to re-engage students. As we teach, it's important that we actively observe our own lessons and the students' response to the lessons. That's how we rethink instructional practice to re-engage students. It's not easy; rethinking takes time and frequent do-overs. The path to re-engagement and maintaining engagement can take many turns, and missteps are to be expected. So embrace the rethinking and redoing process as a celebration of the skills and knowledges that teaching demands of those who have chosen this profession. It's tough, but we can do it.

The branding for Absolut vodka—"Doing things differently leads to something exceptional"—celebrates the use of thinking about product development outside of established practice. As educators, we can encourage this sort of thinking about what it means to be different. Since there may be some truth to the fact that a student is not doing the same work as his or her classmates, approach this conversation with honesty. There's no point in trying to convince the student otherwise. Respond in a way that acknowledges the student's concerns, but also makes the path forward clear and do-able. Here's an example:

"The educator showed me what I had in me." (Cooperider, 2008)

You may notice that now, but I have information about what you can do, and it's my job to find lessons that will move you forward. It's your job to work hard so you can see how you are learning more and more. You should be able to notice your progress, but if you don't, let me know and we'll rethink what we're doing. I'm always here to answer your questions.

Developing Student Independence

It's important that your lessons be planned to develop student independence. Re-engaging the disengaged student is not about providing compensatory instruction. A well-planned lesson for any student matches the student's "zone of proximal development," and is delivered using a model of gradual release of responsibility so that the student's independence can emerge.

The "gradual release of responsibility" (Routman, 2002) is an empowering concept for both educator and student. This concept acknowledges the important role of the educator in the careful planning of lessons that scaffold on student learning and then lead the student to independence. The educator knows when to lead, and also when to diminish and fade out that leadership. During the fading, the student's independence emerges.

A lesson that leads to independence is carefully planned to provide just the right amount of challenge. This level of challenge was referred to by Vygotsky as "the zone of proximal development." The zone of proximal development is

> the distance between the actual development level as determined by independent problem solving and the level of potential development as determined through problem solving under adult guidance or in collaboration with more capable peers. (Vygotsky, 1978)

Knowing When to Stop Talking

In the template on page 75, the Procedures section cautions against talking too much. I think that overtalking a lesson is a common trait among teachers—it is certainly something I'm guilty of. We are trying to ensure that our students have clarity on the topic of the lesson. But overtalking doesn't provide clarity; it often creates confusion or loss of interest.

Think about your own reaction when a lecturer (or author!) talks and talks and talks. My guess is that you begin to fade out. Luckily, you often know enough about the subject that you can fill in the missing pieces. That's not true for many students; when they fade out, key elements of information are missed and gaps occur. There's an interesting phenomena common among students who have the tendency to "fade out" of a lesson: in an attempt to fill in the missing pieces, the student connects the pieces of information he or she does have into what seems to be a coherent sequence or story line. It's often a story line that has little application to the actual lesson. That's why, when we ask some students to retell the information of the day's lesson, the retelling seems so far removed from the original that we often wonder, "Where did that come from?"

A disengaged student might have learned to tune out teacher talk, or to wait until all the talk is over and then ask, "What are we supposed to do?" This is frustrating for any educator, but rather than reacting to the annoyance, try taking this question as a cue. It might be time to rethink the amount of teacher talk.

A clear message of the lesson's topic, a reason why the lesson is being taught (e.g., "I noticed that you can... , now we'll move on to..."), and a real-world application of how the information can be used provides a clear starting point. The talk related to the lesson can always be condensed, and the presentation format of the lesson should be varied to include more than talk.

I'll be the first to fess up to too much talking. During the introductory preamble to an assignment I gave my Grade 2 class, I went on at length about their task. They were to research a personal hero and display that research as a picture. All students appeared to be very engaged in the visual format of the assignment and the results were mostly very good. Mostly. I received drawings that provided evidence of the students' research into heroic figures such as the ones shown on the next pages:

Jonas Salk

Nelson Mandela

Grandmother who cared for children

Dr. Martin Luther King

Mother Teresa

I also received these drawings:

My apartment

My bus stop

As the students described these last two drawings to me, it became clear that they had both tuned out of the lesson and had re-engaged only when they heard something of interest—the words "draw a picture." I had taken their engagement in drawing the picture as an indication that they were responding to my lesson, when it was simply the opportunity to draw that engaged them. It was clearly a case of an educator (me) talking, but not listening or observing. I learned a lot from that experience.

Meeting Teaching Challenges

Despite our best attempts to re-engage students, it's not always an easy path. There will be noncompliant students. Noncompliance might be demonstrated in quiet resistance, in overt displays of oppositional behavior, or by anything in between. For the educator of a noncompliant student, it's often difficult to weed through the outward expressions of noncompliance—the lack of completed work, the minimal quantity of work, the student comments about how pointless the assignment is (the ever-present, "This sucks!")—to find something positive that is worth commenting on and building on. But it's there. If a teacher knows the student as a person—as a learner—there will be evidence of a place to start. Whatever the quality or quantity of work, whatever interest level, it's a start. We ask "questions that carry assumptions of competence, capability" (Lord, 2007) and we move on from that point. The expectations we have of the disengaged student, which are actually higher than the expectations for the rest of the class (remember, there's a lot of ground to make up), are built in from this start point. Our job is to create the how-to lessons that make the expectations attainable.

We also know that some students come from very difficult circumstances; some short-term, some long-term. The stories of the challenges faced by students are legion. As educators, it's our role to provide a space and time for students to know that who they are and what they bring to the learning situation are valued. As educators, it's the best of what we do.

In his role as a social worker, my father had regular conversations with people facing difficult circumstances. One conversation stayed with him always. In this conversation, a man was reflecting on his life and the difficulties he had faced. He said repeatedly, "It was hard, yes, it was hard, all my life it was hard." When my father asked this man if there was any one person that he felt had made his life a little less hard, he responded without a moment's hesitation: "Yes, my teacher, Mrs. _____. She made me feel like I was somebody. She knew me and she told me I could do so much more. But she was the only one." Kids from difficult circumstances need to know that there will be more than one Mrs. _____ in their life. Each teacher has the potential to be one of those people.

Debate Graphic Organizer

Debate Topic:

Step 1. What I already know about this topic:

Pros	Cons

Step 2. Extra Information from my group members:

Pros	Cons

Step 3. More information from articles, online research, etc.:

Pros	Cons

Step 4. After considering all of the above, my strongest arguments are…

Pros	Cons

Pembroke Publishers © 2010 *Engaging the DisEngaged* by Beth Critchley Charlton ISBN 978-1-55138-258-6

Connection Collection Template

Pembroke Publishers © 2010 *Engaging the DisEngaged* by Beth Critchley Charlton ISBN 978-1-55138-258-6

Interest Bank Graphic Organizer

You've told me that you have an interest in _____. When did that interest begin?	Can you describe something about _____ that you just can't forget?	What's something about _____ that you really like?	What's something about _____ you really don't like?
Who is a _____ that you respect? Why?	What is something that you'd like to change about _____ (in the world, in your life, in school)?	Is there a recent controversy in _____? Tell us about it.	Fill in your choice of information here.

Pembroke Publishers © 2010 *Engaging the DisEngaged* by Beth Critchley Charlton ISBN 978-1-55138-258-6

Planning Next-Steps Instruction

Date:	

Individual Lesson:	Group Lesson:
Whole-class lesson:	

What do I know about the student(s)?

Next-Steps Lesson Focus:

Text/Materials Needed:

Procedure:

Assessment of Assignment:

Notes:

Pembroke Publishers © 2010 *Engaging the DisEngaged* by Beth Critchley Charlton ISBN 978-1-55138-258-6

Conclusion: Going Beyond What You Know

"Every kid was good at something, and the trick was to find out what it was, then use it to teach him everything else. It was good work, the kind of work that let you sleep soundly at night and, when you awoke, look forward to the day." (Walls, 2009)

Throughout this book, our focus has been on re-engaging the disengaged learner by answering the question, "What do you know?"

We've discussed the perspective through which we come to know a student and all he or she brings to the schooling process. It's a perspective that looks first for the actual and then for the possible. The actual is the student's foundation of knowledge; the possible leads us to plan next-steps lessons with a purpose and content that the student can "see himself or herself" in. By identifying with the content and the purpose, the student sees the lessons as an invitation to engagement.

Once students accept the invitation, the lessons provide them with the thinking and problem-solving tools that allow them to see learning as a process and not as a set of skills to be remembered. As the lessons continue, we listen, make careful observations, record careful notes, and have thoughtful teacher–student conversations to ensure that ongoing success is evident to the educator and is felt by the student.

This focus requires a rethinking of some of our practices. The first step of rethinking is to ask the same question of our practice that we use to inform our observations of our students: "What do you know?" That question leads us to our own solid foundation. We value this knowledge and move forward to our own next steps.

An educator's next steps involve ongoing research, discussions with colleagues, courses, and reading. Our colleagues in education are irreplaceable, and the profession of teaching should be honored for the wealth of information encompassed within the four walls of every school.

As we continue with the rethinking process, we keep an open mind and approach each new piece of research, each discussion with colleagues, and each professional development session with questions—not defensive questions; rather, questions that lead to insight. The more we question, the more we know and the more we can build our practice. Our rethinking allows us to challenge misconceptions about students, teaching, and educational philosophy with knowledge rather than simple reaction. This knowledge is our power and it's important that we use it. That's how we remain engaged in our profession.

And it's also this knowledge that allows us to put into perspective the ever-present "solutions" to disengagement that inundate the popular press and professional journals. These solutions—a new program, new funding, a new school, financial rewards, financial penalties, or new administrative personnel—are quick fixes and have as much staying power as any other quick fix; that is to say, not much.

Rethinking our practice takes time, patience, and constant reflection on what we've accomplished and where we're going next. We need the knowledge, and sometimes the courage, to think through educational fads and search for the elements that have staying power. Those are the elements that lead to re-establishing the wonder of learning and the ongoing success of the learner.

While rethinking, we should remember those who influenced us and make every attempt to define their influence. Remembering the words or lessons of a favorite educator from our own pasts, a parent, a relative, a colleague, or a friend leads us to the realization that those who had the most influence on us knew how to choose the right word or the right actions to connect with us as people. By defining that influence, we realize that it's these connections that lead us forward and provide us with the ability to influence our students in the same way.

Recently, I've had conversations with several retired educators who spoke of letters they received from former students, many of whom had entered their classrooms as disengaged students and left as engaged students. While each letter was carefully composed to reflect the influence of each specific educator, it was obvious that all letters carried the same message: "You were my teacher and you made a difference because you knew me and you cared." Those words speak of knowing, trust, and re-engagement. What greater praise can there be?

Acknowledgments

We often ask our students to reflect on what they've read. Our purpose is to gather information about the depth to which each student understands and applies the content of the text. As we read the students' reflections, we realize that our students can give us new insights into well-known material.

This book is my own reflection about the research I've read, the research I've conducted, the experiences I've shared, and the conversations I've had about teaching and learning. I'm heavily indebted to those whose words and actions I've read, observed, and shared. All have led me to new insights and understandings. From supper-table and road-trip conversations to educational conferences featuring internationally renowned speakers, each experience has informed my interest in seeing what is possible and my believe in the importance of acting on that possibility.

Many thanks to my professional colleagues, my teachers, and my friends, all who have contributed to this reflection. But most all, thank you to my students. It is through you that I have learned the most.

Bibliography

Atwell, N. (1998) *In the Middle: New Understandings About Writing, Reading and Learning.* Portsmouth NH: Heinemann.

Bainbridge, J., Heydon, R., Malicky, G., Lang, L. (2009) *Constructing Meaning.* Toronto, ON: Nelson.

Clay, M. (1991) *Becoming Literate: The construction of inner control.* Portsmouth, NH: Heinemann.

Clay, M. (2000) *Running Records for Classroom Teachers.* Portsmouth, NH: Heinemann.

Cooperider, D. (2008) *The Appreciative Inquiry Handbook.* San Francisco, CA: Berrett Koehlers.

Costa, A., Kallick, B. (2000) "Activating and Engaging Habits of Mind" ASCD, September.

Council of Minister's of Education in Canada (CMEC) *National and International Learning Assessment Activities,* ACDME 95-CMEC 97 B.4 Appendix II

Creators Project at http://www.thecreatorsproject.com/

Critchley, D. (1992) *How Many Times Must a Man Turn His Head.* Bermuda: Island Press.

Daniels, P. "My Best Educator" in *TES Magazine,* March 2010.

Davis, K. (2008) *Trust in the Lives of Young People: A conceptual framework to explore how youth make trust judgments.* (Good Work Project Report Series No. 52). Cambridge, MA: Harvard University, Project Zero.

Duke, N.K., Pearson, D. (2002) "Effective Practices for Developing Reading Comprehension" in *What Research Has to Say About Reading,* International Reading Association.

Garcia, S.B., Guerra, P.L. "Deconstructing Deficit Thinking: Working With Educators to Create More Equitable Learning Environments" in *Education and Urban Society,* Vol. 36, No. 2, 2004.

Kohl, H. (1994) *I Won't Learn From You and Other Thoughts on Creative Maladjustment.* New York, NY: WW Norton & Co.

Leighteizer, V. K. "Resistance Reconceptualized" in *Paideusis,* Vol. 16, No. 1, 2006.

Lord, J. (2007) *What Kind of World Do You Want?* (self-published) Lord and McAllister.

Moll, L.C., Amanat, C., Neff, D., Gonzalez, N. "Funds of Knowledge for Teaching: Using a Qualitative Approach to Connect Homes and Classroom Theory into Practice" in *Qualitative Issues in Educational Research,* Vol. 31, No. 2, Spring 1992, pp. 132–141

Principles for Fair Student Assessment Practices for Education in Canada at http://www2.education.ualberta.ca/educ/psych/crame/files/eng_prin.pdf

Ramirez, A., Carpenter, D. "Challenging the Assumptions About the Achievement Gap" in *Educational Leadership*, April 2005.

Routman, R. (2002) *Reading Essentials: The Specifics You Need to Teach Reading Well*. Portsmouth NH: Heinemann.

Sadowski, M. "Putting the 'Boy Crisis' in Context" in *Harvard Educational Review*, Vol. 26, No. 4, 2010.

Sanacore, J., Palumbo, A. "Understanding the Fourth Grade Slump: Our Point of View" in *The Educational Forum, Phi Delta Kappan*, vol. 73, 2009.

Scherer, M. "Do Students Care About Learning? A Conversation with Csikszentmihalyi" in *Educational Leadership* Volume 60, Number 1, September 2002, pp. 12–17.

Sonnenschein, S., Stapleton, L., Benson, L. "The Relation Between the Type and Amount of Instruction and Growth in Children's Reading Competencies" in *American Educational Research Journal*, Vol. 47, No. 2, 2010.

TED (Technology, Entertainment and Design) at http://www.ted.com/

Tomlinson, C.A. "Learning to Love Assessment" in *Educational Leadership*, Vol. 65, 2008.

Van den Bergh, L., Denessen, E., Hornstra, L., Voeten, M., Holland, R.W. "The Implicit Prejudiced Attitudes of Educators: Relations to Educator Expectations and the Ethnic Achievement Gap" in *American Educational Research Journal*, Vol. 47, No. 2, 2010.

Vygotsky, L.S. (1978) *Mind in Society,* edited by Michael Cole, Vera John-Steiner, Sylvia Scribner, and Ellen Souberman. Cambridge, MA: Harvard University Press.

Walls, J. (2009) *Half Broke Horses*. New York, NY: Scribner.

Wood, D., Bruner, J., Ross, G. "The Role of Tutoring in Problem Solving" in *Journal of Child Psychology and Psychiatry*, Vol. 17, 1976.

Index